Mexican Cook Book

By the Editors of Sunset Books and Sunset Magazine

Lane Publishing Co.• Menlo Park, California

Mexican Cooking...It's Easy and Fun

With this cook book and some ingredients readily available in most supermarkets, you can easily prepare your favorite dishes from south of the border—and enjoy yourself immensely in the process. Recipes include everything from antojitos (appetizers) to flans (wonderful Mexican custard desserts), plus a variety of gazpachos, tacos, enchiladas, and tamales in between. In addition you'll find many Mexican dishes you may not have discovered yet, information on chiles and other special ingredients, drinks such as sangrias and margaritas to cool the palate, and suggestions on foods that go well together.

Sunset's first Mexican Cook Book sold over a million copies, thus contributing to a better understanding of Mexican cuisine in other parts of the world. In this edition are longtime favorite recipes, plus newer ones discovered by Sunset's food editors on scouting trips to Mexico. Included for the first time are color photographs to stimulate your appetite by giving you closeup views of specific dishes, and to pique your imagination by showing dramatic but practical settings for entertaining Mexican-style. For her help in staging these photographs, a special thank you to Lynne B. Morrall. We are also grateful to Kay Jimenez for her helpful advice and consultation on Spanish terminology and pronunciation.

Edited by: Jerry Anne DiVecchio

Judith A. Gaulke

Special Consultant: Joan Griffiths

Photography: Glenn M. Christiansen

Illustrations: Ward Schumacher

Design: Steve Reinisch

Cover: Create a Fiesta Tostada (page 23) for any occasion. Layers of beans, beef and cheese form the base for a pyramid of refreshing garnishes: shredded iceberg lettuce, tomato wedges, avocado slices, red onion rings, guacamole (page 9), and sour cream. Fan with tortilla chips and top with a mild red pickled pepper. Serve Salsa Cruda (page 62) and lime wedges to enliven the flavor. Photographed by Darrow M. Watt. Cover design: Lynne B. Morrall.

Editor, Sunset Books: David E. Clark

Sixth printing February 1983

Contents

A Tour of Mexican Foods

Synonymous with fiestas, gaiety, and color, Mexican food conjures up images of happy diners being serenaded by strumming mariachi bands under a canopy of stars and purple bougainvillea.

Foods of Mexico *are* festive, colorful, healthful, and easy to make, and they certainly do invite attractive staging for entertaining. But they also can be enjoyed in everyday menus— consider, for example, huevos rancheros for breakfast (page 47), tostadas for lunch (page 23), and carne asada for dinner (page 31).

Contrary to popular belief, Mexican food doesn't have to be hot. Seasonings can be delicate or bold at the discretion of the cook. Our recipes give ample leeway in determining seasoning levels— in fact, most are on the mild side, making them totally in tune with American eating habits.

Mexican dishes were not devised by chefs with delicate palates. Originally, many dishes were improvised by natives who had simple cooking facilities and no refrigeration, and who needed to use what food they had on hand— corn, beans, rice, and chiles.

Now, refined by practice and modern conveniences, Mexican dishes have taken on flair but without losing their identifiable features— tortillas, chile or tomato sauce, rice, corn, and beans in one form or another.

Americans are always surprised to find restaurants in Mexico offering few of the familiar tacos, tostadas, and tamales normally served in American-Mexican restaurants. Instead, roasted meats, fish, poultry, and stews are common menu entrées, usually served with rice and beans.

Tacos and tostadas, on the other hand, are considered snacks in Mexico and they're sold by street vendors to passersby. As the tourist quickly learns, snacking is the favorite Mexican pasttime, sustaining the populace until the customary late dinner hour of Mexico— from 8 o'clock on.

No special cooking utensils or implements are required to use this book unless you want to make your own corn or flour tortillas. For this, a tortilla press is helpful but not necessary. Simple directions for building your own wooden press are on page 74, or you may prefer to purchase the metal kind.

Serving from colorful Mexican pottery can add an authentic touch to any meal. Our photographs suggest ways of serving your meals.

Shopping for Mexican ingredients

In the bustling open-air markets of Mexico, fresh produce is heaped high in a mad, colorful, aromatic array—papayas as large as melons, gigantic pineapples, and both red and yellow bananas in a variety of sizes are common sights.

Some of Mexico's less familiar produce items are becoming more available in our grocery stores and gourmet food departments. Look for jicama, the large brown turnip-shaped root with its appealing white, crisp flesh you can enjoy raw or in many cooked dishes; or any number of fresh and dried chile peppers; or fresh coriander (cilantro), the herb with large, parsleylike leaves.

You may have to poke around your supermarket to locate Mexican products—tortillas are usually in a refrigerated case; canned green chiles may be with olives and pickles; Mexican red chile sauce and taco sauce are often near tomato sauce and paste; and Mexican chocolate might be on the candy shelf.

For your reference and familiarity, what follows is a description of the more popular food products used in this book.

Beans. Beans appear at every Mexican meal, and a bubbling pot of beans is omnipresent in the Mexican kitchen. Served as a starchy accompaniment, they are mashed as refried beans and offered as a filling or topping for other dishes. Dried pink, red, pinto, black, and kidney beans are all popular. In some cases, canned beans make an easy short cut.

Cheese. Mexicans use a cheese that melts well and is similar to jack cheese or Longhorn Cheddar. In this book, recipes that call for cheese usually specify one or the other.

Chiles. Detailed information appears on page 6—even directions for drying your own.

Chile sauces. Chiles are the key ingredient in a variety of canned and bottled sauces: taco sauce (red or green), Mexican red chile sauce (not to be confused with the bottled cocktail chili sauce), enchilada sauce, green chile salsa, and jalapeña salsa. Recipes for some homemade varieties are on pages 62 and 63.

Chili powder. Spice companies market their own blends of chili powder, usually consisting of ground dried chiles and other seasonings. In Mexican stores, powders of just-dried chiles are sold, ranging from mild to sweet to very hot. Paprika is a powder of mild, sweet chile.

To make your own chili powder, start with dried chiles (directions for drying are on page 6). The hotness will vary with the chiles you use. To make 1/2 cup chili powder, you'll need about 3 ounces dried chiles—use mild chile peppers, such as pasilla or Anaheim, or a combination of mild and hot peppers. Pull off and discard stems and seeds. Break up pods and whirl in a blender until finely ground to make 1/3 cup. (Avoid breathing powder or getting it in your eyes. It can severely irritate delicate membranes.) Mix chile with 1 tablespoon ground cumin, 2 teaspoons salt, 1 teaspoon *each* ground allspice, garlic powder, and ground oregano, and 1/2 teaspoon *each* ground cloves and coriander. Store airtight.

Chorizo. These spicy, seasoned sausages, usually sold in link form, are used throughout this book as a filling for many dishes. Bulk chorizo (page 64) can usually be substituted for purchased chorizo in our recipes.

Coriander (**cilantro**). Fresh coriander looks like large, lacy parsley. But it has its own spicy, pungent aroma and flavor. You may find it under the name of Chinese parsley when sold in Oriental markets.

To grow your own coriander, use whole coriander seed found on the spice shelf. Sow seeds 1/4 inch deep in rows 6 inches apart. Water soil lightly and keep damp until seeds sprout (usually within 2 weeks). Encourage new growth by cutting off young tender leaves and stems as you would pick parsley.

Jicama. This brown-skinned root vegetable is shaped something like a turnip but varies in size—from 3 or 4 inches to a foot or more in diameter. Just peel off the thick skin—inside, the white, crisp meat looks like a potato and tastes like a water chestnut; use it raw or cooked.

Masa harina (dehydrated masa flour). Specially prepared corn flour (sometimes called corn tortilla or tamale flour or instant masa) is used to make tortillas and tamales. A large part of the dehydrated masa flour sold in major metropolitan areas and throughout the western and southwestern United States is made by the Quaker Oats Company. The registered trademark name of that product is Masa Harina, used throughout this book.

Tomatillo. These little, green, tart tomatoes about the size of a walnut are covered with a parchmentlike skin that is stripped away to expose the fruit. Different in flavor from the green version of an ordinary tomato, the pulp is very dense and has tiny seeds. Tomatillos are readily available canned.

Tortillas. Corn or flour tortillas, the traditional round, flat bread of Mexico, are available in supermarkets, or you can make them at home (pages 73 and 74). They can be toasted, heated, fried, cut up, rolled, folded, or made into tortilla chips.

Chiles—some like them hot

Perhaps the chief misconception about chiles is their red-hot reputation. Many *are* fiery hot, but many others are sweet, mild, or richly flavored. Their hotness is concentrated in the interior veins or ribs near the seed heart, not in the seeds as is commonly believed. (The seeds taste extra hot because they are in close contact with the hot veins.) If, when the pepper is cut open, the veins have a yellowish orange color in that area, it usually indicates the pepper will be a potent one.

Use caution in handling and storing chiles. When using large amounts of fresh or dried chile peppers, wear gloves to protect your hands because the oil, capsaicin, in the peppers can cause severe burns. Don't touch your face or eyes. If chiles do come in contact with your bare hands, wash thoroughly with soapy water. Similarly, when you're grinding your own chiles, be careful in removing the lid from the blender container, as fine powder will get into the air and can burn eyes and nose.

More than 140 varieties of chiles are grown in Mexico alone. Those that follow are most popular in the United States and used in recipes throughout this book.

The spelling of "chile" is used here as it is used by Mexicans. Because American spice companies label their ground chile blends "chili," you will encounter that spelling in recipes using the purchased ground spice.

To dry your own chiles, tie the stems onto a sturdy piece of twine, placing chiles close together and making the strand as long as you wish. Hang in a dry area with air circulating freely around the strand. In several weeks, chiles lose their brilliant hue, changing to a deep, glistening red; they will feel smooth and dry.

Ancho. This chile looks and tastes very much like an ordinary bell pepper but can be considerably more peppery at times. Tapered rather than square, it is firmer, less crisp, more waxy-looking. It turns a bright red and sweetens up in fall. When dry, it assumes a flat, round shape and wrinkles up like a prune.

Bell peppers. Probably the most familiar pepper in the United States, the green and red bell peppers are squarish and fist-size. Green peppers turn red in the fall, becoming sweeter and milder, yet retaining their crisp, firm texture.

California green chiles (Anaheim). Fresh, these peppers are 5 to 8 inches long, 1^1/$_2$ to 2 inches wide, tapering to a point, usually a bright, shiny green. The flavor ranges from mild and sweet to moderately hot. To use fresh peppers, peel the skin from the chiles using the process described on page 11. Canned California green chiles (whole or diced) are readily available in the United States. When using fresh or canned, taste for hotness—they can vary greatly from pepper to pepper.

Fresno chiles. Bright green, changing to orange and red when fully matured, Fresno chiles have a conical shape—about 2 inches long and 1 inch in diameter at the stem end. They are often just labeled "hot chile peppers" when canned or bottled.

Jalapeño chiles. These peppers have thicker flesh, darker green color, and a more cylindrical shape than Fresno chiles; however, the heat level of the two varieties is about the same—hot! Canned and bottled peppers are sometimes labeled "hot peppers" with jalapeño as a subtitle. They are also available in sauce form as salsa jalapeña, and pickled.

Pasilla. The true pasilla is a long, thin pepper 7 to 12 inches long by 1 inch in diameter. Pasillas turn from dark green to dark brown as they mature.

Pimentos. These heart-shaped chiles are purchased canned in the United States. The flesh is softer and a little sweeter than the common red bell pepper.

Serrano. Dynamite-hot is an understatement for these tiny 1-inch peppers. When new on the vine, they are rich, waxy green, changing to orange and red as they mature. They are also sold canned, pickled, or packed in oil.

Small, whole, red dried hot chiles. Labeled this way on supermarket spice shelves, many small, tapered chiles about 1 to 2 inches long are sold dried, but there is no one varietal name that applies to all of them.

Yellow chiles. Many short conical-shaped yellow peppers with a waxy sheen go by this name— Santa Fe grande, caribe, banana pepper, Hungarian, Armenian way, floral gem, and goldspike. Probably most familiar are the canned pickled wax peppers. Their flavor ranges from medium-hot to hot.

Appetizers and Snacks

Antojitos and party foods

Mexicans are accustomed to snacking whenever they're hungry— so it's no wonder that a variety of tidbits suitable for appetizers is typical of the cuisine.

In fact, some of the foods served as main dishes by restaurants in the United States are eaten mainly as snacks or appetizers in Mexico. The well-known tacos are a prime example. Tacos are sold by street vendors for between-meal eating, and they may even be prepared over a charcoal brazier at the most posh cocktail party by someone hired for the task. (We have a special chapter on tacos, page 24.)

Appetite-creating or appetite-sating foods are called "antojos" (whims), or "antojitos" (little whims), depending on their size.

To turn them into party appetizers, the cook may simply serve them in smaller quantity or greater variety— or make them in a smaller size. Tamales prepared in miniature are called "tamalitos" (little tamales, page 52). The meat-filled turnovers, "empanadas," are likewise called by the diminutive, "empanaditas" (page 29), when made in diminutive size.

Refried Bean Dip

Aperitivo de Frijoles Refritos
(ah-pe-ree-*tee*-voh deh free-*hoh*-less rrreh-*free*-tohs)

Perfect for a large party, this dip will serve a crowd. It is laced with Cheddar cheese and green onion and can be kept hot over a candle warmer.

2 cups refried beans (page 68 or canned)
1 cup (about 4 oz.) shredded Cheddar cheese
½ cup chopped green onion, including some tops
¼ teaspoon salt
2 to 3 tablespoons taco sauce
Tortilla chips (page 77 or purchased)

In a pan or heatproof Mexican pottery bowl, mix together refried beans, cheese, onion, salt, and taco sauce. Cook, uncovered, over low heat, stirring, until heated. Keep warm over a candle warmer; serve with tortilla chips to dip. Makes about 3 cups.

Guacamole

(guah-kah-*moh*-leh)
Avocado Dip

Even someone who is indifferent to avocado in other forms is likely to become an avid guacamole fan. To make this Mexican favorite, you mash avocado and then mix it with a choice of seasonings to serve as a dip with chips. You can also use it as a sauce for meats and main dishes, as a dressing for salads, or as a filling for tortillas. (See photograph on page 38.)

2 large ripe avocados
2 to 3 tablespoons lemon or lime juice
Salt
1 to 2 tablespoons chopped fresh coriander (cilantro) or about ½ teaspoon ground coriander (optional)
2 to 4 canned California green chiles (rinsed, seeded, and chopped) *and/or* cayenne, liquid hot pepper seasoning, or minced hot green chiles (jalapeño, serrano, and others) to taste
Tortilla chips (page 77 or purchased)

Cut avocados in half, remove pits, and scoop out pulp with a spoon; or peel. Mash pulp coarsely with a fork while blending in lemon or lime juice. Add salt to taste and coriander, if desired. Add chopped chiles, cayenne, or hot pepper seasoning for a touch of heat. Serve with tortilla chips to dip. Makes about 1²/₃ cups.

Variations. Add 1 clove **garlic** (minced or pressed) or 2 or 3 tablespoons minced **onion**— or use both garlic and onion. Add 1 large **tomato**, chopped (peeled and seeded, if desired). Blend **mayonnaise** into mixture for a smoother consistency. Mix in 1 **pimento**, chopped.

Garnish with **tomato wedges** and fresh **coriander** (cilantro) or **parsley sprigs**, or sprinkle **pomegranate seeds** over top.

Oaxacan Peanuts

Cacahuetes (kah-kah-*ooeh*-tehs)

These nuts improve with standing, especially if they're stirred occasionally. The Mexicans use whole peeled garlic and leave it with the peanuts, but our version avoids the risk of losing a friend who eats a clove of garlic instead of a peanut.

20 small dried red chiles (serrano chiles or others about 1 inch long)
4 cloves garlic, minced or pressed
2 tablespoons olive oil
2 pounds salted peanuts
1 teaspoon coarse salt (use a salt mill or buy kosher salt)
1 teaspoon chili powder

In a pan over medium heat, cook chiles, garlic, and oil for 1 minute, stirring so chiles won't scorch.

Mix in peanuts and stir over medium heat; or spread on baking sheet and bake in a 350° oven for 5 minutes or until slightly brown.

Sprinkle with coarse salt and chili powder. Mix well, cool, and then store in airtight container for at least 1 day before serving. (They keep well up to 2 weeks.) Makes 7 cups.

Roasted Pumpkin Seeds

Semillas Tostadas de Calabaza
(seh-*mee*-yas tohs-*tah*-thas deh kah-la-*ba*-sah)

Pale green, crunchy, and nutlike, pumpkin seeds are a traditional Mexican snack. You don't have to wait for a Halloween pumpkin to obtain pumpkin seeds. They are available, hulled, in natural food or health food stores. Roast them flavored with salt or one of the suggested seasonings. If you buy the seeds in quantity you can store them raw in the freezer.

1⅓ cups water
3 tablespoons salt
½ pound (1²/₃ cups) raw hulled pumpkin seeds

(Continued on next page)

Bring water and salt to a boil; stir until salt is completely dissolved. Pour over pumpkin seeds in a bowl. Cover and let stand at room temperature for 12 to 24 hours.

Drain liquid from seeds. Spread seeds evenly over a 10 by 15-inch shallow-rimmed baking pan. Bake, uncovered, in a 350° oven for 25 to 35 minutes, stirring frequently (seeds that soak for 24 hours require maximum time) or until seeds are dry and puffed (kernel separates in center). Let cool, stirring occasionally. Store airtight. Roasted pumpkin seeds stay fresh up to 10 days. Makes 1²/₃ cups.

Flavored pumpkin seeds. Follow directions for roasted pumpkin seeds, but omit the 3 tablespoons salt from boiling water. Drain soaked seeds and sprinkle with 2 teaspoons of **onion salt** or **garlic salt**, or with 3/4 teaspoon *each* **chili powder** and **salt**; mix until well distributed. Bake as in preceding directions.

Jicama Appetizer

Jicama Fresca (*hee*-kah-mah *fres*-kah)

Jicama, a crisp root vegetable, is sold as a snack by street vendors in Mexico. Cut in thin slices, it has a crunchy texture that resembles a water chestnut.

> 1 tablespoon salt
> ¼ teaspoon chili powder
> 1 to 2 pounds jicama, peeled
> 1 lime, cut in wedges

Blend salt with chili powder and put in a small bowl. Slice jicama in about 1/4-inch-thick slices and arrange on a serving tray with lime wedges and bowl of seasoned salt.

To eat, rub jicama with lime, then dip in salt. Makes 4 to 8 servings.

Nachos

(*nah*-chos)
Tortilla Chips with Melted Cheese

Cheese melts over corn chips heated quickly in the oven. Guests pull apart individual chips to eat with their fingers.

> 6 to 8 cups tortilla chips (page 77 or purchased)
> 4 cups (about 1 lb.) shredded jack or mild Cheddar cheese (or half of each)
> 1 can (4 oz.) whole California green chiles (for mildest flavor, remove seeds and pith), chopped

Spread tortilla chips equally about one layer deep (they overlap) in 2 shallow-rimmed 10 or 11-inch baking pans or ovenproof plates. Sprinkle tortillas evenly with cheese, then chiles.

Place both pans, uncovered, in a 400° oven for about 5 minutes or until cheese melts (or bake in sequence so you can replenish the first serving with another hot one). Serve at once, picking up tortilla pieces with your fingers; if desired, keep nachos hot on an electric warming tray. Makes 6 to 8 servings.

Tortilla Appetizers

Tostadas de Harina (tohs-*tah*-thas *deh* ah-*ree*-nah)

Flour tortillas make a crisp, tasty base for these hot appetizers. You can also serve them as accompaniments for soup or salad.

> ¾ pound chorizo (purchased), skinned, or 1½ cups bulk chorizo (page 64) or ½ can (12-oz. size) corned beef
> 6 flour tortillas (page 74 or purchased)
> 2 cups (about 8 oz.) shredded mild Cheddar cheese
> 2 tablespoons seeded, chopped, canned California green chiles

Crumble meat into a wide frying pan and cook over medium heat, stirring, until lightly browned; drain and discard fat.

Evenly sprinkle tortillas with shredded cheese, leaving about 1/2-inch margin around edges. Top with cooked chorizo or corned beef, and chiles.

Arrange on ungreased baking sheets and bake in a 425° oven for 8 to 10 minutes or until edges are crisp and browned. Cut each tortilla into 6 wedges; serve hot. Makes 3 dozen.

Grilled Cheese

Queso al Horno (*keh*-soh ahl *or*-noh)

Grill cheese over very low coals on a miniature barbecue, such as a Japanese hibachi. If your fire is too hot, the cheese will burn on the bottom and boil over. When it has completely melted, remove it from the fire; return the cheese to the heat occasionally to keep it warm and melted as it is served.

> 1 to 1¼ pounds jack cheese
> 12 corn tortillas (page 74 or purchased)
> About 1½ cups tomato and green chile sauce (page 62) or canned green chile salsa

Slice cheese in 1/4-inch-thick slices; place a single layer in an 8-inch heatproof dish. Cover and set aside.

Heat tortillas by placing them, one at a time, on a medium-hot griddle or in an ungreased wide frying pan over medium-high heat; heat for about 30 seconds on a side or just until soft. Stack tortillas and cut in quarters. Wrap in a tea towel or foil and keep warm until serving time.

Place plate of cheese to melt over *very low* charcoal fire. Have guests make their own appetizers by spreading some of the softened cheese on a tortilla wedge, spooning on a little chile sauce, then folding tortilla wedge to enclose filling. Makes about 48 appetizers.

Chiles with Cheese

Chile con Queso
(*chee*-leh kohn *keh*-soh)

This spicy dip can lead a double life, serving also as a sauce to spoon over meat, eggs, or hot vegetables.

  2 tablespoons salad oil
  2 medium-size onions, chopped
  12 to 16 fresh California green chiles, peeled (directions follow); or 2 cans (7 oz. *each*) whole California green chiles, seeded and chopped; or 2 cans (7 oz. *each*) diced green chiles
  1 teaspoon salt
  1 small can (5 oz.) evaporated milk
  2 cups (about 8 oz.) shredded jack or Longhorn Cheddar cheese
  Tortilla chips (page 77 or purchased)

In a 2-quart pan, heat salad oil over medium heat; add onions and cook until onions are very soft. Add chiles

and salt and cook, stirring, until juices have evaporated (about 5 minutes). Add evaporated milk and cook gently, stirring, until slightly thickened (about 4 minutes).

Remove from heat, cool about 2 minutes, add cheese, and cover until cheese melts. Then stir and serve hot.

When using as a dip, keep warm over candle warmer and serve with tortilla chips. Makes about 4 cups.

How to use fresh green chiles. Wash and wipe dry. Arrange peppers close together in a broiler pan; place 1 inch below heat in a preheated broiler. Turn often until blistered and lightly browned all over. As done, drop chiles into a plastic bag; close bag. When cool enough to handle, peel off loose skin with a knife; leave any small pieces that refuse to come off easily. For a milder flavor, cut chile open and remove seeds. Chop enough to make 2 cups.

Little Tortillas with Pork

Panuchos
(pah-*noo*-chos)

A specialty from the Yucatan, panuchos are eaten as an appetizer or snack. Small, homemade masa tortillas are fried, then piled high with a black bean paste and chile-seasoned pork mixture, and topped with a garnish. Fun for a patio or pool party, assembled panuchos can be served on a tray, or guests can stack up their own. Tortillas, pork mixture, and bean paste can all be made ahead of time, then reheated before serving.

  Salad oil
  3 pounds well-trimmed pork butt, cut into 1-inch cubes
  3 cloves garlic, minced or pressed
  3 tablespoons chili powder
  ¾ teaspoon *each* ground allspice, ground cumin, crushed red pepper, and salt
  1 teaspoon oregano leaves
  ¼ cup white wine vinegar
  2 cups water
  ⅓ cup finely chopped fresh coriander (cilantro)
  24 small corn tortillas (page 74), crisp-fried (page 76)
  Black bean paste (recipe follows)
  Marinated onion rings (recipe follows)
  Garnishes: 2 large tomatoes, sliced; 3 hard-cooked eggs, sliced; 2 avocados, peeled, pitted, and sliced

Heat 2 tablespoons oil in a wide frying pan set over medium-high heat; add half the pork cubes at a time; cook, turning frequently, until all are well browned.

Add garlic, chili powder, allspice, cumin, red pepper, salt, and oregano to meat and cook, stirring, for 1

 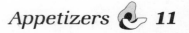

minute. Then add vinegar and water and bring to boiling; reduce heat, cover, and simmer for 1½ hours or until meat is tender enough to fall apart. Break pork cubes into coarse shreds with a wooden spoon; add coriander. Cook, uncovered, for 5 to 10 minutes or until most liquid has evaporated. (Cover and refrigerate if made ahead. Reheat to serve.)

To serve, spread 1 tablespoon bean paste on each tortilla; top with a heaping tablespoon pork, a few drained marinated onion rings, a tomato slice, egg slice, and avocado slice. Makes 2 dozen panuchos.

Black bean paste. Rinse 8 ounces dried **black or red pinto beans**; drain. Place in a 3-quart pan with 5 cups water and 1/2 small **onion**. Cover and cook over low heat for about 2 hours or until beans mash readily with a fork. Turn beans with remaining liquid into a blender and whirl until smooth, stopping and stirring as necessary. (Cover and chill purée if made ahead.)

Before serving, heat 2 tablespoons **salad oil** in a frying pan set over medium heat; add 3 cloves **garlic** (minced or pressed), 1/4 teaspoon **cayenne**, 1 teaspoon **salt**, and **bean purée**. Cook, stirring frequently, for about 2 minutes or until very thick.

Marinated onion rings. Slice 2 small **onions**; separate into rings. With your hands, mix onions with 1 teaspoon **salt** until soft. Rinse and drain thoroughly. Place in a small bowl with 1/2 teaspoon **salt**, 1 teaspoon **oregano leaves**, 1/3 cup **white wine vinegar**, and 2/3 cup **water**. Stir to coat thoroughly; cover and chill for at least 4 hours or as long as 2 days. Drain thoroughly before spooning onto tortillas.

Shellfish Cocktail

Mariscos
(mah-*rees*-kohs)

Chunks of succulent scallops or bright pink shrimp are marinated in piquant lime juice and served as a first course.

1½ pounds raw scallops or medium-size
    deveined, shelled, and cooked shrimp
1½ cups water
¼ teaspoon grated lime peel
¼ cup *each* lime juice and dry white wine
½ cup catsup
3 or 4 drops liquid hot pepper seasoning
   Salt and pepper

If scallops are used, first poach them in simmering water, just until they lose their translucence throughout (about 8 to 10 minutes).

Place cooked scallops or shrimp in a deep bowl. Mix together lime peel and juice, wine, catsup, and hot pepper seasoning; pour over seafood. Mix well and season with salt and pepper to taste. Cover and chill

well before serving. Serve in chilled cocktail or sherbet glasses. Makes 6 to 8 servings.

Fish Appetizer, Acapulco-style

Seviche de Acapulco (seh-*vee*-cheh deh ah-kah-*pool*-koh)

Seviche, a popular appetizer in Mexico, is made from raw fish or shellfish marinated in lime or lemon juice. The seafood looks and tastes as though it has been poached. It is white and firm and has lost any raw, translucent look.

1½ pounds mild-flavored fish fillets (such as sole
    or halibut) or raw scallops
1 cup lemon or lime juice (about 5 lemons or 6
   limes)
2 canned California green chiles, seeded and
   chopped
½ cup minced onion
2 large tomatoes, peeled, seeded, and chopped
1 teaspoon salt
¼ teaspoon oregano leaves, crumbled
¼ cup olive oil
   Garnishes: avocado slices, canned California
    green chiles (cut in strips), pimento strips,
    chopped fresh coriander (cilantro)

Cut fish in small, thin pieces; if scallops are used, dice or thinly slice them. Place in a bowl, stir in lemon or lime juice, and refrigerate for 2 hours.

Stir in chiles, onion, tomatoes, salt, oregano, and olive oil.

Serve in chilled cocktail or sherbet glasses. Top with one or two of the suggested garnishes. Makes 8 to 12 servings.

Soups and Colorful Salads
Gazpacho to tostadas

Soup is an important part of the "comida," the big meal of the day. The soup that begins a comida usually is a light one. But Mexican soups run the gamut from clear broths to rib-sticking concoctions of several meats and vegetables to which fresh vegetable relishes may also be added at serving time. Cream soups of a light nature are often served, too.

Offered right after the soup course at the comida may be another dish called a "sopa seca" (dry soup), if the meal is a fiesta or a formal occasion. But they aren't soups at all and would not be served as such in an American-style meal. They are rice, pasta, hominy, or other starchy dishes comparable to the pasta or pilaf courses served in other countries with little or no liquid. Find dry soups in the chapter on vegetables and rice.

The soups on the following pages are soupy in the way you would expect. Several are filling enough to be main dishes if served with plenty of soft, hot tortillas or tortilla chips.

Salads are not an important part of Mexican cuisine—vegetable salads, particularly the mixed green type, are rarely seen. Chile peppers and tomatoes are used in abundance, though, and many dishes are garnished with chopped lettuce or avocado.

What we propose here as whole-meal salads are tostadas, topopas, and chalupas, in which tortillas or corn cakes and shredded lettuce form the framework for a variety of vegetable and meat additions.

With any Mexican meal, crisp raw vegetable relishes, olives, and pickled peppers—presented on a bed of crushed ice, if you like—may be all the salad you need.

Sonorese Corn Soup

Sopa Sonorense (*soh*-pah soh-noh-*ren*-suh)

Named for the state of Sonora, this soup is based on chicken broth plus a mingling of the sweet, mild flavors of green pepper, corn, and chili powder. Whipped cream piled onto the hot soup just before serving dissolves deliciously into each portion.

    2 tablespoons butter or margarine
    1 teaspoon chili powder
    2 cups seeded and diced green bell pepper
    2 cans (12 oz. *each*) whole kernel corn with red
        and green sweet peppers, drained
    1 small, dry, whole hot red pepper
    6 cups regular-strength chicken broth
        Salt
    1 cup whipping cream
    ¼ teaspoon salt

Melt butter in pan and stir in chili powder and green pepper. Cook, uncovered, stirring, over medium heat for about 3 minutes. Add corn, red pepper, and broth and bring to a boil, still uncovered. Reduce heat and simmer for about 3 minutes; salt to taste, if needed; remove red pepper.

Whip cream with the 1/4 teaspoon salt until stiff. Pour soup into tureen and pile whipped cream on top. Stir slightly and ladle mixture from bottom of dish (the corn settles) into individual bowls. Makes 8 to 10 first-course servings.

Asparagus with Cream Cheese

Caldo de Exparrago con Queso
(*kahl*-doh deh es-*pah*-rrrah-goh kohn *keh*-soh)

To this typical light soup of asparagus pieces cooked in chicken broth, you have the option of adding chunks of cream cheese or spoonfuls of cool, thick sour cream.

    1 package (10 oz.) frozen cut asparagus
    4 cups regular-strength chicken broth
        Salt
    2 small packages (3 oz. *each*) cream cheese or
        1 cup sour cream

Combine asparagus and broth in a pan and bring to boiling, uncovered. Stir to break asparagus apart; then reduce heat and simmer gently, uncovered, for 10 minutes. Add salt to taste, if needed.

Cut cream cheese into about 1/2-inch cubes and place in a soup tureen. Pour in hot asparagus soup

and serve at once. (Or instead of using cream cheese, pass sour cream to spoon onto individual servings of soup.) Makes 6 to 8 first-course servings.

Pork & Hominy Soup

Pozole (poh-*soh*-leh)

Pozole, laced with chunks of ham and hominy, is complemented by a topping of shredded lettuce and fried tortilla strips.

    2 large cans (47 oz. *each*) regular-strength
        chicken broth
    3 pounds ham hocks
    1 pound bony chicken pieces (wings, backs, or
        necks)
    2 medium-size onions, cut in pieces
    1 teaspoon oregano leaves
    ½ teaspoon cumin seed
    1 large can (1 lb. 13 oz.) golden hominy, drained
    2 or 3 limes, cut in wedges
        Fresh tomato salsa (recipe follows)
    2 small packages (3 oz. *each*) cream cheese,
        diced
    1 jar (7½ oz.) sweet roasted red peppers, diced,
        or 1 to 1½ cups seeded and diced red bell
        pepper
    2 cups thinly shredded iceberg lettuce
    1 to 1½ cups thinly sliced green onion,
        including some tops
    4 to 6 corn tortillas (page 74 or purchased), cut
        in strips and fried (page 77)

In an 8-quart kettle, combine broth, ham, chicken, onion, oregano, and cumin. Cover and bring to a boil, then reduce heat and simmer gently for 1 hour. Pour broth through a wire strainer and return to kettle. Cover and chill stock. Discard skin and bones from ham; wrap and chill meat. Also discard chicken and vegetables.

Lift off solidified fat, return ham to stock, add hominy; cover and simmer gently for 30 minutes.

Serve soup hot, offering individual bowls of lime wedges, tomato salsa, cream cheese, red peppers, lettuce, green onion, and tortilla strips. Makes 8 to 10 main-dish servings.

Fresh tomato salsa. Peel, seed, and chop 2 medium-size **tomatoes.** Remove seeds from 1 or 2 canned **California green chiles** and chop; combine with tomatoes (and juices) and 1/2 cup chopped **onion.**

Tomato-Pepper Cream Soup

Caldo Largo (*kal*-doh *lar*-goh)

From La Paz on the Baja coast comes this version of caldo largo. Caldo is the word for broth, but largo generally means "long." It's a puzzle how a soup can be long, so one of the other meanings of the word may be intended, perhaps "abundant." All ingredients for this soup are indeed abundant and usually on hand in any Baja kitchen.

Another explanation for the name might be that the soup was originally made with the largo variety of chile, a long pepper.

    2 tablespoons salad oil
    2 medium-size tomatoes, peeled, seeded, and
        diced
    2 medium-size green bell peppers, seeded and
        cut in thin strips
 1½ cups regular-strength chicken broth
    1 can (13 oz.) evaporated milk
        Salt
        Liquid hot pepper seasoning
    ¼ pound jack cheese, diced

Heat oil in a wide frying pan over medium heat; add tomatoes and peppers, and cook until peppers are limp. Add broth and simmer, uncovered, for about 10 minutes. Stir in milk; add salt and hot pepper seasoning to taste. Mix in cheese and ladle soup immediately into bowls. Makes 4 to 6 first-course servings.

Xochilt Broth

Caldo Xochilt (*kal*-doh so-*chee*-tleh)

To chile-seasoned brown stock, you add avocado, tomato, onion, and lime. The special dried ancho chile used in this soup is generally available in Mexican markets or delicatessens, but you can substitute crushed red pepper found on supermarket spice shelves.

    1 large, dry, whole ancho chile, stem and seeds
        removed, or ¼ teaspoon crushed red pepper
        Boiling water
    6 cups regular-strength beef broth
    2 tablespoons rice
    ⅓ cup canned garbanzos, drained
    1 medium-size tomato, peeled and chopped
    1 canned California green chile, seeded and
        chopped
    1 medium-size onion, chopped
        Salt
    1 ripe avocado, peeled, pitted, and diced
    ⅓ cup chopped fresh coriander (cilantro)
    2 limes, cut in wedges

In a large pan, cover ancho chile (if used) with boiling water and let stand for 10 minutes. Drain and cut into small pieces. In same pan, combine beef broth, chile, rice, and garbanzos. Bring to a boil, reduce heat, cover, and simmer for about 20 minutes or until rice is tender.

Blend tomato, California chile, and 1/4 cup of the chopped onion with salt to taste. Place remaining onion, tomato mixture, and avocado in individual serving dishes.

Remove soup from heat and stir in coriander. Ladle soup into bowls, adding onion, tomato, and avocado as you like; squeeze lime juice over to taste. Makes 6 first-course servings.

Black Bean Soup

Sopa de Frijoles Negros (*soh*-pah deh free-*hoh*-les *neh*-gros)

Look for black kidney beans in markets that stock Mexican or Oriental foods, or in health food stores. These beans, about 3/8 inch long, resemble our red kidney bean in shape, but are ebony in color.

The soup is generously laden with ham chunks. Serve with lemon slices and a dollop of sour cream.

    1 pound (2¼ cups) dried black kidney beans
 2½ quarts water
    1 pound ham hocks, cracked
    2 stalks celery, chopped
    2 cloves garlic, minced or pressed
    2 large onions, chopped
    ½ teaspoon pepper
    ¼ teaspoon ground allspice
    1 tablespoon beef stock base or 3 beef bouillon
        cubes
    1 can (8 oz.) tomato sauce
    ½ cup dry red wine or 3 tablespoons lemon juice
        Salt
    1 lemon, thinly sliced
        About 2 cups sour cream

(Continued on next page)

. . . Black Bean Soup (cont'd.)

Rinse and sort beans, discarding any foreign material. Combine beans and water in a 5-quart kettle and bring to a boil for 2 minutes, then cover and set aside for 1 hour. Add ham (in one or several pieces), celery, garlic, onion, pepper, allspice, and beef stock base. Cover and simmer for 2 to 3 hours or until beans mash readily.

Remove ham and set aside; then stir tomato sauce and wine into beans. Whirl part of the soup at a time in a blender until smooth, then return puréed beans to pan. Dice ham (discard bones and skin) and return to soup. Season with salt to taste. Reheat soup to boiling and serve with lemon slices on top. Pass sour cream to spoon onto each serving. Makes about 6 main-dish servings.

Guadalajara Soup

Sopa de Guadalajara (soh-pa deh
guah-tha-la-*hah*-rah)

Sturdy enough to be a main course, this soup can be prepared in make-ahead steps that are a plus for the cook with little time. Condiments, added at the table, give liveliness to the flavorful pork and bean brew.

3½ to 4-pound boneless pork shoulder
1 tablespoon salad oil
1 cup finely chopped onion
2 cloves garlic, minced or pressed
2 teaspoons chili powder
1 teaspoon *each* oregano leaves and cumin
    seed
7 cups water
2 cans (14 oz. *each*) regular-strength beef broth
1 cup dried pinto or small red beans
4 cups thinly sliced carrots
2 jars (about 4 oz. *each*) baby corn on the cob,
    drained
    Salt and pepper
    Condiments (suggestions follow)

Trim excess fat from meat and cut meat into 1 to 1½-inch cubes. In a 5-quart kettle, heat oil over medium-high heat; add meat and brown well on all sides. Push to sides of pan, add onion and garlic, and sauté until limp. Stir in chili powder, oregano, cumin, water, broth, and beans. Cover and simmer for about 1½ hours or until meat and beans are tender to bite. (This much can be done ahead; cover and chill.)

Skim fat from broth (or, if chilled, lift off solidified fat). Heat broth to boiling; reduce heat, add carrots, cover, and simmer until carrots are fork tender (about 30 minutes). Stir in corn and add salt and pepper to taste. Pour into a soup tureen or serving bowl and serve with condiments. Makes 6 to 8 main-dish servings.

Condiments. Pass individual bowls of **cherry tomato** halves, sliced **green onions**, chopped fresh

coriander leaves (cilantro), and **sour cream**; also offer **lime** wedges and bottled **jalapeña salsa.**

Clear Gazpacho

Gazpacho Simple (gahs-*pah*-cho *seem*-ple)

Different from the more familiar tomato-colored soup, this gazpacho is broth-based and clear. Serve it in an ice liner made by inserting a smaller serving bowl into an ice-filled larger bowl. Offer condiments on the side. (See photograph on page 19.)

6 medium-size tomatoes, peeled and chopped
2½ quarts regular-strength chicken broth
1 tablespoon wine vinegar
½ teaspoon oregano leaves, crumbled
1½ tablespoons olive oil
    Salt
1 avocado, peeled, pitted, and sliced
    Condiments (suggestions follow)

In a soup tureen or clear glass bowl (at least 3-qt. size) set in a larger bowl of shaved ice, mix tomatoes, broth, wine vinegar, oregano, oil, and salt to taste. Chill, if made ahead.

Before serving add avocado slices to soup. Serve condiments, each in a separate container, to add to individual servings according to personal preference. Makes 8 to 10 first-course servings.

Condiments. Offer 1 to 1½ cups chopped **green onion** (including some tops) or mild onion; 1 to 1½ cups salted **almonds**; 1 to 2 cups chopped **watercress** (including some stems) or fresh coriander (cilantro); 2 peeled, pitted, and chopped **avocados** (sprinkled with **lemon** or lime juice to preserve color); 2 or 3 **limes**, cut in wedges; coarse **salt.**

Tomato Gazpacho

Gazpacho de Tomate
(gahs-*pah*-cho deh to-*mah*-teh)

For a more traditional gazpacho, use chilled tomato juice for a quick, colorful soup studded with diced vegetables. To keep it cold, add ice cubes to individual bowls.

½ cucumber, peeled or unpeeled
½ mild red or white onion
½ avocado, peeled, pitted, and sliced or
    chopped
½ teaspoon oregano leaves, crumbled
3 tablespoons olive oil or salad oil
2 tablespoons wine vinegar
4 cups canned tomato juice
    Ice cubes
2 limes, cut in wedges

Cut off a few slices of cucumber and onion; save for garnish. Chop remaining cucumber and onion in small pieces. Put onion, cucumber, avocado, oregano, oil, and vinegar into a tureen or serving bowl. Stir in tomato juice. Top with reserved cucumber and onion slices; chill.

    Ladle into individual bowls, adding 2 or 3 ice cubes and lime juice to taste. Makes 6 first-course servings.

Tripe & Hominy Soup

Menudo (meh-*noo*-doh)

Menudo is a soup of tripe and corn in some form, most often made from dried corn. Canned hominy makes a good substitute.

    The soup traditionally is served on the eve of Christmas or New Year's. Mexican men out on the town stop at all-night cafes for a menudo nightcap, because a bowlful is said to be good preventive medicine for hangovers.

5 pounds tripe
1 large veal knuckle
4 large cloves garlic, minced or pressed
1 tablespoon salt
2 cups chopped onion
1 teaspoon minced fresh coriander (cilantro)
1 tablespoon chili powder (or to taste) or 1 can
    (4 oz.) California green chiles, seeded and
    chopped
    About 4 quarts water
1 large can (1 lb. 13 oz.) golden hominy, drained
2 tablespoons lemon juice
2 cups chopped green onion, including some
    tops
1½ cups chopped fresh coriander (cilantro) or
    fresh mint

Cut tripe in oblong pieces or slivers. Put in an 8-quart kettle with veal, garlic, salt, onion, the 1 teaspoon coriander, chili powder, and water. Cover and simmer for about 6 hours or until tripe is fork tender, adding more water if necessary. Remove and discard knuckle.

    Add hominy and heat until hot through; then add lemon juice. Serve with green onion and coriander to spoon into individual servings. Makes 6 to 8 main-dish servings.

Meatball Soup

Sopa de Albondigas
(*soh*-pa deh al-*bohn*-dee-gahs)

Moist meatballs poach in stock with gold and green vegetables. Fresh lime juice accents each serving.

1½ pounds lean ground beef
¼ cup all-purpose flour, unsifted
2 eggs
1 large can (47 oz.) regular-strength chicken
    broth
3 cans (10½ oz. *each*) condensed consommé
1 teaspoon oregano leaves
2 medium-size onions, chopped
1 large, dry, whole ancho or pasilla chile,
    seeded and crumbled, or 1 small, dry, whole
    hot red chile, seeded
6 carrots, very thinly sliced
¼ cup rice
¼ to ⅓ cup chopped fresh coriander (cilantro)
¾ pound spinach
2 to 3 limes, cut in wedges

Combine beef, flour, eggs, and 1/2 cup of the broth. In an 8-quart kettle bring remaining broth, consomme, oregano, onions, and chile to boil; reduce heat to low. Quickly shape meat mixture into balls about 1½ inches in diameter; as shaped, drop into stock. Simmer meatballs, uncovered, for 5 minutes, then spoon off any fat and foam from surface. Add carrots, rice, and coriander. Simmer, uncovered, for 20 minutes or until carrots and rice are tender to bite.

    Meanwhile, discard spinach stems; wash leaves well, then cut crosswise into thin shreds. Add spinach to stock and cook, uncovered, 5 minutes longer. Ladle into wide soup plates or bowls. Pass lime to squeeze over all. Makes 6 to 8 main-dish servings.

 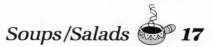

Salads

Clear gazpacho is a surprise—instead of a chilled tomato-based soup, this one starts with chicken broth, and diners add any number of condiments. Recipe is on page 16.

Orange Salad

Ensalada de Naranjas
(en-sah-*la*-thah deh nah-*rahn*-has)

Marinated slices of orange and onion are spiced with chili powder. (See photograph on page 38.)

  5 large oranges, peeled and sliced
  1 large mild red onion, thinly sliced
  ⅓ cup salad oil
  ¼ cup wine vinegar
  1 teaspoon sugar
  ½ teaspoon salt
  ¼ teaspoon chili powder
    Paprika
    Crisp butter lettuce leaves
    Whole black pitted olives

Arrange orange and onion slices alternately in layers in a bowl. Mix together oil, vinegar, sugar, salt, and chili powder; pour over salad. Sprinkle with paprika. Serve on lettuce leaves. Garnish with olives. Makes 8 servings.

Jicama Pico de Gallo

Pico de Gallo con Jicama
(*pee*-koh deh *gah*-yoh kohn *hee*-kah-mah)

The most typical pico de gallo contains the sweet, crunchy, water chestnut-like root, jicama.

  2 cups peeled and diced raw jicama
  1 green bell pepper, seeded and slivered
  ½ medium-size mild onion, thinly sliced
  1 cup sliced or diced cucumber
  ¼ cup olive oil
  2 tablespoons white or red wine vinegar
  ½ teaspoon oregano leaves, crumbled
    Salt and pepper

Combine jicama, green pepper, onion, and cucumber. Mix together oil, vinegar, and oregano; pour over vegetables and mix lightly. Add salt and pepper to taste. Makes 4 to 6 servings.

Orange Pico de Gallo

Pico de Gallo Naranjas
(*pee*-koh deh *gah*-yoh nah-*rahn*-has)

There are many versions of pico de gallo made with a variety of ingredients, usually chopped or cut into chunks. The name—meaning "rooster's bill"—refers to the old-style way of eating the salad by picking up the chunks with the fingers, which resembles the way a rooster pecks corn.

In this version, the cut-up ingredients are served over a bed of romaine, making forks preferable to fingers.

  2 quarts crisp, bite-size pieces romaine
  1 medium-size orange, peeled and thinly sliced
  ½ cucumber, thinly sliced
  ½ mild red onion, thinly sliced
  ½ green bell pepper, seeded and diced
  ½ to 1 cup peeled and chopped raw jicama or
      sliced water chestnuts
  ½ cup salad oil or olive oil
  ½ cup wine vinegar
  ½ teaspoon salt
    Small romaine leaves (optional)

Place lettuce in a salad bowl. Decoratively arrange orange, cucumber, onion, green pepper, and jicama over top.

Blend oil with wine vinegar and salt. Pour dressing over salad and mix lightly to serve. Garnish rim of salad with tips of inner romaine leaves, if you like. Makes 8 servings.

Marinated Tomatillo Salad

Ensalada de tomatillo
(en-sah-*la*-thah deh toh-mah-*tee*-yoh)

Looking and tasting like little tart green tomatoes, tomatillos add spark to a salad.

Combine 8 fresh or canned **tomatillos** (husks removed and fruit sliced), 2 medium-size **tomatoes** (sliced), 1 medium-size **cucumber** (sliced), and 1 small **red onion** (thinly sliced). Stir together 2 tablespoons **white wine vinegar**, 6 tablespoons **olive oil**, 1 teaspoon **sugar**, 1/2 teaspoon **dry basil**, 1/4 teaspoon **salt**, and 1/8 teaspoon **pepper**. Pour over vegetables.

(Continued on page 20)

Cover and chill at least 30 minutes or up to 2 hours. Makes 4 to 6 servings.

Christmas Eve Salad

Ensalada de Nochebuena
(en-sah-*la*-thah deh *noh*-cheh-booeh-nah)

After Christmas Eve mass or the midnight hour comes a supper that traditionally includes this salad and one of several classic turkey dishes.

    1 medium-size head iceberg lettuce, shredded
    8 small cooked beets, peeled and thinly sliced
    4 oranges, peeled and thinly sliced
    4 unpeeled red apples, cored and thinly sliced
    4 bananas, thinly sliced
    1 pineapple, peeled, cored, and thinly sliced; or
        1 can (1 lb. 14 oz.) pineapple chunks, drained
    3 limes, peeled and thinly sliced
    ¼ cup sugar (optional)
      Seeds of 2 pomegranates
    1 cup salted peanuts, chopped
    ½ cup salad oil
    ¼ cup red wine vinegar
      Salt

Put lettuce in large shallow bowl and arrange beets, oranges, apples, bananas, pineapple, and limes over it, sprinkling with sugar if sweetness is desired. Sprinkle pomegranate seeds and peanuts over all.

Mix oil with vinegar and salt to taste. Just before serving, pour over salad and mix. Makes 8 servings.

Kidney Bean Salad

Ensalada de Frijoles
(en-sah-*la*-thah deh free-*hoh*-less)

There's an interesting texture play in this salad: crisp celery, crunchy nuts, and meaty beans. Though you can prepare it a day in advance, it will be crisper if you assemble it just a few hours ahead.

    1 can (about 1 lb.) red kidney beans
    2 cups chopped celery
    1 tablespoon minced onion
    ½ cup chopped walnuts
    4 small sweet pickles, chopped
    ¼ cup salad oil
    3 tablespoons wine vinegar
    ½ teaspoon *each* salt and pepper
      Lettuce (optional)

Drain beans thoroughly; combine with celery, onion, nuts, and pickles. Mix oil, vinegar, salt, and pepper; pour over bean mixture; toss. Serve on lettuce, if you wish. Makes 6 to 8 servings.

Marinated Beef Salad

Carne a la Vinagreta (kar-*nee* a la vee-nah-*greh*-tah)

Cooks in many countries make leftover meat into a salad by cutting it into strips and marinating it in a vinaigrette sauce. The Mexican version is simple but has imaginative seasoning.

    4 cups cooked lean beef, cut in strips
    1 large onion, thinly sliced
    2 tablespoons *each* capers and minced parsley
    ½ cup olive oil
    ¼ cup wine vinegar
    1 teaspoon *each* oregano leaves, crumbled, and
        prepared mustard
    ½ teaspoon salt
      Lettuce leaves

Put meat strips on a rimmed platter and cover with sliced onion. Sprinkle with capers and parsley. Mix together oil, vinegar, oregano, mustard, and salt. Pour over meat, cover, and chill for at least 3 hours to blend flavors. Serve on lettuce leaves. Makes 4 to 6 servings.

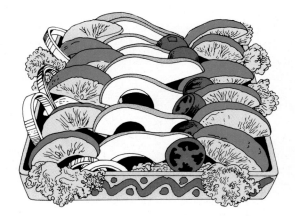

Mayan Salad

Ensalada Maya (en-sah-*la*-tha *maee*-ya)

Spicy Mexican main dishes benefit from a crunchy, cooling salad companion. For greens, use iceberg or butter lettuce, romaine, or spinach; or present a combination of two or three.

    2 quarts crisp greens, torn into bite-size pieces
    1½ cups jicama (cut in julienne strips) or sliced
        water chestnuts
    1 medium-size mild red onion, sliced
    1 grapefruit
    2 oranges
    ½ pound cherry tomatoes, halved
      Cumin dressing (recipe follows)
    1 large avocado

Mix greens and jicama in large salad bowl; arrange onion rings on top. Peel grapefruit and oranges, remove all white membrane from sections, and arrange sections atop onions along with tomatoes. Cover; chill for 1 to 2 hours. Meanwhile, make cumin dressing; set aside.

To serve, peel, pit, and slice avocado; arrange on salad. Pour over dressing and mix gently. Makes 6 to 8 servings.

Cumin dressing. In a blender, combine 3 tablespoons **cider vinegar**, 2 tablespoons fresh **lime juice**, 6 tablespoons **olive oil** or salad oil, 1 clove **garlic**, 1 teaspoon **black pepper**, 1/2 teaspoon *each* **salt** and ground **cumin**, and 1/8 teaspoon crushed **red pepper**. Cover; whirl until well blended.

Mexican Chef's Salad

Topopo (toh-*poh*-poh)

A counterpart for our hearty chef's salad, topopo takes the much more dramatic shape of a mountain or volcano. Because this main-dish salad is typical of the cuisine shared by the northern state of Sonora and next-door Arizona, it reflects tastes on both sides of the border.

    2 corn tortillas (page 74 or purchased),
        crisp-fried (page 76)
    About ½ cup refried beans (page 68 or
        canned), heated
    Topopo lettuce layer (directions follow)
    8 to 12 cold cooked large shrimp, shelled,
        deveined, and cut in half lengthwise; or
        about 1 cup cold sliced cooked turkey or
        chicken
    1 avocado, pitted, peeled, and sliced lengthwise
    About ¼ cup diced Longhorn or mild Cheddar
        cheese
    1 canned California green chile, seeded and
        chopped
    ¼ cup shredded or grated Romano cheese
    Tomato wedges or canned jalapeño chiles

Spread each tortilla with half the beans, covering completely. Place tortilla in a rimmed serving dish (about dinner plate size). Mound half the lettuce onto it to create a mountain shape.

Arrange half the shrimp, chicken, or turkey around sides of salad, then fill in with half the avocado slices. Sprinkle or place Longhorn cheese and California green chile over salad. Spoon Romano cheese on salad and top with tomato wedges or jalapeño chiles. Serve at once. Makes 2 topopos.

Topopo lettuce layer. Mix 1 cup cold cooked **peas** (or thawed frozen petit peas) with 1 teaspoon minced canned **jalapeño chile** (seeds and pith removed), 1/2

cup chopped **green onion**, 4 to 5 cups finely shredded **iceberg lettuce**, 1/4 cup **salad oil**, 2 tablespoons **vinegar**, and **salt** to taste.

Chalupas

Chalupas (cha-*loo*-pahs)

By the curious logic that characterizes the naming of Mexican dishes, a chalupa can be anything that starts with a masa pancake—the base that distinguishes this towering salad.

    ¼ cup butter or margarine, at room temperature
    1½ cups masa harina (dehydrated masa flour)
    ½ teaspoon salt
      About ¾ cup water
    2 tablespoons salad oil
    1 medium-size onion, chopped
    1 can (8 oz.) tomato sauce
      About 1 bottle (7 oz.) red taco sauce
      About 3 cups cooked diced chicken or turkey
    2 cups refried beans (page 68 or canned)
    1 large clove garlic, minced or pressed
    1 cup (about 4 oz.) shredded Cheddar or jack
        cheese
      Guacamole (page 9 or purchased)
      Condiments (suggestions follow)

To prepare masa dough, put butter in small bowl of electric mixer and beat until fluffy. Mix in masa flour, salt, and water; beat until dough holds together well, adding a little more water if needed.

Divide dough into 5 equal parts and pat each out on wax paper to a 5-inch circle. (If you do this ahead, stack with wax paper between, wrap well, and refrigerate until next day.)

Heat oil in a wide frying pan over medium heat; add onion and cook until golden. Add tomato sauce and about 1/4 cup of the taco sauce, or to taste. Simmer, uncovered, stirring often, until thickened slightly (about 5 minutes). Remove from heat, stir in chicken or turkey, and turn into a 1 or 1½-quart casserole; cover and set aside. (Cover and chill if made ahead.)

In a shallow baking dish, combine beans, garlic, 2 tablespoons of the taco sauce, and cheese; mix well. Set dish, uncovered, in a 325° oven. Place covered casserole of chicken in oven at same time. Bake both dishes for 30 to 40 minutes or until heated through, stirring several times. Prepare guacamole, put it in a serving dish, cover, and chill.

Heat a wide ungreased frying pan or griddle on medium heat (about 350° on electric griddle). Flip masa dough off paper onto ungreased griddle and fry until light brown (about 3 minutes on each side). Stack fried cakes on foil, wrap, and place in oven with beans and chicken to keep warm.

Assemble chalupas by spreading fried cakes with
(Continued on page 23)

 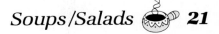

Build a whole-meal tostada salad as high as you like, starting with a crisp-fried tortilla and adding on from there (recipe below).

. . . Chalupas (cont'd.)

guacamole, and adding hot refried beans and a pile of chicken in its spicy sauce. Offer remaining taco sauce and condiments in separate bowls to top individual servings. Makes 5 servings.

Condiments. Pass individual bowls of shredded **iceberg lettuce** (about 3 cups), **sour cream with chives** (about 1 cup), thinly sliced **green onions** and tops, pitted ripe **olives**, and coarsely chopped fresh **coriander** (cilantro).

Tostadas

(tohs-*tah*-thas)

A whole crisp-fried tortilla makes the bottom layer — then meats and cheese are piled high. The ingredients traditionally offer contrasts of soft and crisp, hot and cold, sharp and mild. (See photograph at left. Fiesta Tostada pictured on front cover.)

    4 to 5 cups shredded iceberg lettuce
    4 corn tortillas (page 74 or purchased),
        crisp-fried (page 76)
    1 cup refried beans (page 68 or canned), heated
    ½ cup (about 2 oz.) shredded jack or Cheddar
        cheese
      About 1 cup slivered cooked chicken, turkey,
        or pork; or 1 cup ground beef filling (page
        64)
      Garnishes: Egg slices, tomato wedges, onion
        rings, avocado slices or guacamole (page 9 or
        purchased), sour cream, chopped green onion,
        Mexican red chile sauce (page 62 or canned),
        tortilla chips (page 79 or purchased)

For each tostada, spread a layer of shredded lettuce over a dinner plate. Add a fried tortilla. Spread with about 3 to 4 tablespoons hot refried beans, sprinkle with about 2 tablespoons cheese, cover with 2 or 3 tablespoons meat, top with 1/4 to 1/2 cup more shredded lettuce, garnish with a few slices of egg, tomato wedges, onion rings, avocado slices (or about 3 tablespoons guacamole), a dollop of sour cream, a sprinkling of chopped green onion, and chile sauce. Makes 4 tostadas.

Fiesta Tostada. Place 3 crisp-fried **corn tortillas** (pages 74 and 76, or purchased) on a shallow-rimmed 10 or 11-inch ovenproof plate (they will overlap). Spread with 1/2 cup heated **refried beans** (page 68 or canned). Cover with 3/4 cup **ground beef filling** (page 64).

Sprinkle with 1/2 cup shredded **Cheddar or jack cheese.** Bake, uncovered, in a 400° oven for 10 to 15 minutes, or until very hot throughout. Remove plate from oven and quickly top with 1 cup shredded **iceberg lettuce.** Choose garnishes from suggestions above. Serve immediately. Makes 4 appetizer or 2 entree servings.

Crab Tostadas

Tostadas de Cangrejo
(tohs-*tah*-thas deh kahn-*greh*-hoh)

Crab and Cheddar cheese are natural partners. Here a crisp tortilla sits atop a bed of greens and takes a mound of fillings.

    1 avocado, peeled and pitted
    2 tablespoons lime juice
    ¼ teaspoon garlic salt
    1 large head iceberg lettuce
    2½ cups refried beans (page 68 or canned)
      4 corn tortillas (page 74 or purchased),
        crisp-fried (page 76)
    1 cup (about 4 oz.) shredded mild Cheddar
        cheese
    ¾ to 1 pound cooked crab
    2 medium-size tomatoes, sliced
    ½ cup pitted ripe olives
      Canned or bottled taco sauce

Mash avocado and blend with lime juice and garlic salt.

Line four plates with outer lettuce leaves; then finely shred remaining lettuce and mound on plates.

Heat beans until they start to bubble. Arrange a crisp tortilla atop greens and spoon over hot beans. Sprinkle with cheese and cover with a layer of crab (save some for garnish).

Spoon on avocado mixture; garnish with reserved crab, tomato slices, and olives. Pass taco sauce to spoon over all. Makes 4 tostadas.

Avocado Salad

Ensalada de Aguacate
(en-sah-*la*-tha deh ah-gooah-*kah*-teh)

Guacamole, the avocado sauce (page 9) used in so many dishes, can also be served as a salad.

Place shredded or torn **iceberg lettuce** in a bowl, top it with a mound of **guacamole**, and garnish with **tomato wedges**, olives, carrot sticks or curls, and radish roses. Sometimes this salad is served with a French dressing or mayonnaise.

 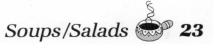

Tacos, Burritos, Sandwiches

Stuffed and filled and fun to eat

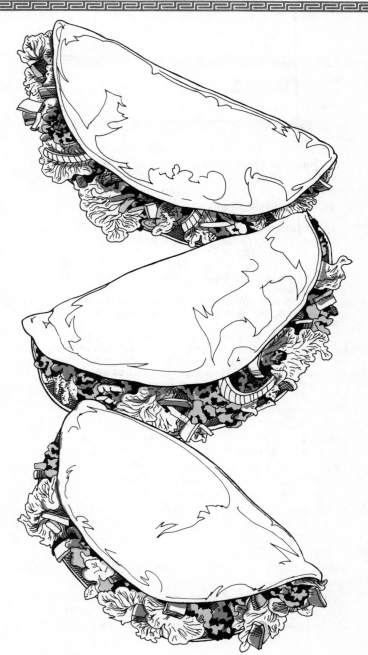

Half-moon-shaped tacos are probably the most popular Mexican food in America. The word taco merely means "snack," and Mexicans enjoy a variety of tacos in soft or fried tortillas either folded or rolled around a filling. In the United States, however, taco generally refers to a crisp-fried corn tortilla folded in half to form a pocket which is then filled with meat, garnish, and spicy sauce.

A burrito, on the other hand, employs a warm, soft flour tortilla to enclose a simple filling, such as refried beans with cheese or scrambled eggs with taco sauce, or a hearty combination of meats (or meat and beans), cheese, sauce, and toppings.

Other snack specialties are really just variations of the taco or burrito. A chimichanga is a flour tortilla, usually a large one, wrapped around any variety of fillings and deep-fried until flaky. Quesadillas contain a cheese filling to which seasoning such as green chiles may be added; the tortilla may be open flat with cheese melted on top, or folded over the cheese. Flautas are made of two overlapping corn tortillas filled and rolled, and fried crisp.

Basic Tacos

(*tah*-kos)

A fried and folded tortilla holding a meat filling, lettuce, cheese, and tomato is the most familiar taco in the United States. For other variations, see the taco tortilla and filling ideas that follow this recipe. (See photograph on page 27.)

> 1 pound lean ground beef
> 1 medium-size onion, finely chopped
> 1½ teaspoons chili powder
> ½ teaspoon *each* oregano leaves and paprika
> ¼ teaspoon *each* dry rosemary, ground cumin, and pepper
> 1 teaspoon garlic salt
> Prepared taco sauce
> 2 teaspoons Worcestershire
> 10 to 12 corn tortillas (page 74 or purchased), crisp-fried and folded (see directions at right)
> About 1 cup (4 oz.) shredded sharp Cheddar cheese
> 2 to 3 cups shredded iceberg lettuce
> 2 large tomatoes, sliced in thin wedges or coarsely chopped

In a wide, ungreased frying pan over medium heat, cook meat until brown and crumbly. Add onion and sauté until limp, then stir in chili powder, oregano, paprika, rosemary, cumin, pepper, garlic salt, 3 tablespoons taco sauce, and Worcestershire. Simmer gently, uncovered, stirring often until hot through.

Fill each fried tortilla with 2 to 3 tablespoons beef mixture. At the table, pass cheese, lettuce, and tomatoes (each in a separate bowl) and additional taco sauce. Makes 10 to 12 tacos.

Taco Tortilla Variations

First decide how you want your taco—soft or crisp-fried, folded or rolled; then decide on the fillings.

Folded or rolled tacos with soft tortillas (corn or flour). For these tacos, you want the tortillas to be piping hot, but still moist and flexible. The easiest way to soften them is to place them individually (not overlapping) on an ungreased medium-hot griddle or in a heavy frying pan over medium-high heat. Turn frequently until soft and hot (about 30 seconds). Wrap in cloth or foil immediately and keep in warm place until ready to use.

Another way to soften tortillas is to moisten your hands with water and rub over each tortilla. Stack and wrap tortillas in foil and place in a 350° oven until steamy (about 15 minutes).

To heat in a microwave oven, wrap tortillas in plastic film or punch several holes in plastic package of purchased tortillas. Cook, allowing 1 to 1½ minutes for 12 tortillas.

To make folded soft tacos, just spoon filling down the center of a hot tortilla, add garnishes and/or sauce, and fold one half of the tortilla over the other to make a semicircular sandwich.

To make rolled tacos, spoon filling slightly off center, roll one side of tortilla over filling, keep rolling until you have a tubular shape.

Folded, crisp-fried tacos. Made with corn tortillas, this is the familiar form sold at taco stands in the United States. (See basic taco recipe at left.)

Heat 1/2 inch salad oil, shortening, or lard in a wide frying pan over medium-high heat to 350° on a deep-fat frying thermometer. When hot, fry one corn or flour tortilla at a time just until tortilla becomes soft (about 10 seconds). Then fold it in half and hold slightly open with tongs or two forks so that there is a space between the halves for filling to be added later. Fry tortilla until crisp and lightly brown, turning as necessary to cook all sides (about 1 minute total).

To keep half-moon-shaped taco shells warm until ready to fill, put them on a paper towel-lined baking sheet in a 200° oven for as long as 10 to 15 minutes.

Rolled, crisp-fried tacos. You can roll, fill, and fry these tacos, or fill the already fried tortillas for a less greasy version.

First soften a corn or flour tortilla by dipping it in hot oil for just a few seconds. Remove, drain on paper towels, and spoon filling slightly off center, down one side of tortilla. Fold small side over filling and roll up.

To hold filling in while you fry taco, secure flap of tortilla with a small skewer or wooden pick, or hold shut with tongs. Fry over medium-high heat in at least 1/2 inch hot salad oil, shortening, or lard until lightly brown and crisp. Drain on paper towels, tilting tortilla so that excess oil can drain out of center.

Some cooks believe it is easier to roll tortillas without filling, fry them, and then fill with a small spoon. This keeps filling from absorbing oil and from falling out during cooking.

Taco Fillings, Sauces, Garnishes

Any innovative combination of fillings, sauces, and garnishes can be used for tacos. Use your imagination to suit your fancy.

For taco fillings you can use any hot cooked meat (ground or shredded) seasoned with taco sauce, taco seasoning mix (sold in foil packets), or onions sautéed in butter or salad oil. Slivers or thin slices of leftover cooked roast meat or fowl also make tasty fillings. A number of enchilada fillings are good for tacos, too. They are bulk chorizo (page 64), pork or chicken (page 64), and "little meats" pork (page 63).

For taco sauces, you can choose from several of the prepared sauces available bottled or canned: taco sauce, canned green chile salsa, or canned Mexican red chile sauce. Or try the homemade sauces in this book: tomato and green chile sauce (page 62), Mexican red chile sauce (page 62), chile-tomato sauce (page 63), and green tomatillo sauce (page 63).

(Continued on next page)

 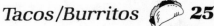

For garnishes, the most popular are shredded lettuce, shredded Cheddar or jack cheese, and chopped tomatoes. Other possibilities include chopped green onions, chopped mild chiles (canned or pickled), sliced or diced avocado, and fresh coriander (cilantro).

Everyone's favorite—the taco—can take several shapes. Traditional crisp-fried, half-moon-shaped tortillas are filled to brim with shredded lettuce, meat, tomato, and cheese. Roll up soft tortillas around same filling for variation. Recipes are on page 25.

Sonora Tacos

Chimichangas (chee-mee-*chan*-gas)

A specialty of the state of Sonora, these are enormous tacos made with platter-size flour tortillas which become flaky when fried. You can make a smaller version with regular-size (7-inch) flour tortillas.

2¼ cups ground meat filling (page 64)
12 flour tortillas (page 74 or purchased)
 Salad oil, shortening, or lard
 Garnishes: 1½ to 2 cups *each* shredded
 Cheddar cheese, shredded lettuce, and
 chopped radishes or green onions

Spoon 3 tablespoons ground meat filling down center of each tortilla. Fold tortillas around filling and fasten with wooden picks. Assemble only 2 or 3 at a time—tortillas will absorb liquid from sauce.

Heat 1 inch oil in wide frying pan over medium heat. Add tortillas, one at a time, turning until golden on all sides (1 to 2 minutes total). With slotted spoon, lift tortilla from oil, drain, then place on a thick layer of paper towels; keep in a warm place until all are cooked.

Serve evenly garnished with 2 or 3 tablespoons *each* shredded cheese, lettuce, and radishes or chopped green onions. Allow 2 or 3 for each serving. Makes 12 chimichangas.

Flute-shaped Tacos

Flautas
(*flou*-tas)

The word "flauta" (flute) describes the tubular shape of this taco variation that uses two overlapping tortillas.

12 corn tortillas (page 74 or purchased)
 About 1½ cups warm meat filling: ground beef
 (page 64), bulk chorizo (page 64), or pork or
 chicken (page 64)
 Salad oil, shortening, or lard

For each flauta, soften and heat 2 tortillas by placing each one on an ungreased griddle over medium-high heat for about 15 seconds on each side. Lay tortillas flat and overlapping.

Spoon a band of 3 to 4 tablespoons warm meat filling across greatest length of the overlapping tortillas, then roll up around filling. Hold shut with tongs (or fasten with small wooden skewers) and, over medium heat in about 1/2 inch oil heated to 350° on a deep-fat frying thermometer, fry until flauta is slightly crisp on all sides. Drain on paper towels. (If you prefer, roll and fry tortillas first, then spoon in filling.) Makes 6 flautas.

Spicy Burritos

Burritos de Carne (boo-*rrree*-tos deh *kar*-neh)

Burritos are warm, soft flour tortillas filled with such savory ingredients as hot and spicy meats, beans, cheese, tomatoes, and green onions. Assemble the makings, then let diners stuff tortillas with any combination they desire. Top with guacamole and sour cream.

 Tomato and chile relish (recipe follows)
 Spicy meat filling or spicy pork filling (recipes
 follow)
 About 18 to 24 flour tortillas (page 74 or
 purchased)
3 cups refried beans (page 68 or purchased),
 heated
 About 3 cups shredded jack cheese (about 12 oz.)
2 cups guacamole (page 9 or purchased)
 About 1 cup sour cream

Prepare tomato and chile relish and chill. Cook your choice of meat filling (reheat if made ahead). Meanwhile, follow directions for reheating tortillas (page 76).

To serve, place relish, meat filling, hot beans, cheese, guacamole, and sour cream in individual bowls. Serve tortillas in towel-lined basket. Let guests make their own burritos by selecting various foods to roll up in the tortilla, then topping burrito with a spoonful of guacamole and sour cream. Makes 18 to 24 burritos or enough for 6 to 8 servings.

Tomato and chile relish. Peel and finely chop 3 or 4 medium-size **tomatoes** to make 3 cups. Stir in 1 cup finely chopped **green onions** (include some tops) and 2 to 4 tablespoons seeded and finely chopped canned **California green chiles**, and 1/2 teaspoon

(Continued on page 28)

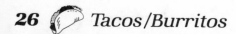

...Spicy Burritos (cont'd.)

each ground **coriander** and **salt**. Cover and chill until ready to serve. Drain off excess liquid before serving.

Spicy meat filling. Heat 2 tablespoons **salad oil** in a wide frying pan over medium heat. Add 1 large **onion** (finely chopped) and 2 cloves **garlic** (minced or pressed). Cook, stirring, until limp. Stir in 4 cups finely diced **cooked meat** (such as beef or pork roast, chicken, or turkey), 1 1/4 cups Mexican **red chile sauce** (page 62 or canned), 1 teaspoon **salt**, 1/2 teaspoon *each* ground **cinnamon** and **cumin**, and 2 to 4 tablespoons seeded, chopped, canned **California green chiles**. Simmer, uncovered, for about 5 minutes.

Spicy pork filling. Cut 3 pounds lean boneless **pork butt** into 1/2-inch cubes. Barely cover with **water**; add 2 cloves **garlic** (minced or pressed) and 1 teaspoon **salt**. Simmer, covered, for 20 minutes; drain well. Place meat on a rimmed baking sheet and drizzle with 1 tablespoon **salad oil**; stir to coat well. Bake, uncovered, in a 400° oven for 20 to 25 minutes or until meat is crisp and browned; stir often.

In a blender, whirl enough small, dried **hot chile peppers** (6 to 12) to make 1 1/2 to 3 teaspoons crushed flakes (or use 1 1/2 to 3 teaspoons crushed red pepper). Also whirl until smooth 1 can (12 or 14 oz.) **tomatillos** and their liquid.

In a 4 or 5-quart kettle, combine meat, tomatillos, 1 can (8 oz.) **tomato sauce**, 1/2 cup **water**, 2 cloves **garlic** (minced or pressed), and **hot chiles** to taste. Cover; simmer until meat is tender when pierced (about 45 minutes).

Party Burritos

Burritos de Fiesta (boo-*rrree*-tos deh fee-*es*-tah)

Assorted pan-fried meats make a deluxe burrito filling, ideal when you're entertaining a few friends. The cooking can all be done ahead, leaving the hostess—or the host—free to enjoy the fun.

    2 dozen flour tortillas (page 74 or purchased)
2½ pounds chicken breasts
1¼ pounds beef top round or sirloin steak
½ teaspoon ground cumin
1 teaspoon salt
2 cloves garlic, minced or pressed
1 pound chorizo (purchased), skinned, or 2
    cups bulk chorizo (page 64)
    Water
2 tablespoons *each* butter or margarine
2 tablespoons olive oil
2 packages (5 oz. *each*) miniature, fully cooked,
    smoked sausage links
6 ounces jack cheese, thinly sliced
2 large mild onions, thinly sliced
    Guacamole (page 9 or purchased)
    Tomato salsa (page 33)

Follow directions for reheating tortillas (page 76).

Remove skin and bones from chicken breasts and slice into 1/2-inch-wide strips. Slice steak on the diagonal 3/8 inch thick, then into 1/2-inch-wide strips. Sprinkle both meats evenly with cumin, salt, and garlic, rubbing in lightly with your fingertips. Place purchased chorizo in a pan, cover with water, and simmer for 10 minutes; drain.

Heat frying pan over high heat, add 1 tablespoon *each* of butter and oil, and lay chicken strips in pan in a single layer. Cook quickly, uncovered, turning, until browned on all sides (about 2 minutes). Remove from pan and arrange in a chafing dish or warm serving pan or dish.

Heat remaining 1 tablespoon *each* butter and oil in frying pan and put in steak strips in a single layer. Cook quickly, uncovered, turning once, until browned on both sides (about 1 minute). Transfer to dish with chicken.

Slice chorizo on diagonal about 1/4 inch thick, or crumble into pan along with smoked sausage, and heat just until hot through. Then arrange in dish with other meats.

Place dish of meats on warming tray. Arrange cheese and onion slices on a plate. Serve guacamole and tomato salsa in bowls. Arrange hot tortillas in a towel-lined basket alongside meats. Makes 24 burritos or enough for 6 to 8 servings.

Chile & Cheese Sandwich

Chiles con Queso Seco
(*chee*-lehs kohn *keh*-soh *seh*-koh)

This spicy-sweet chile and cheese combination served on French bread makes an unusual open-faced sandwich or appetizer. The Mexicans call it chiles con queso seco (chiles with dry cheese) because grated "dry" (hard) cheese (dry jack or Parmesan) is used. The resulting mixture is very moist, nevertheless. You can prepare the cheese mixture or even assemble the sandwiches in advance.

    8 large, dry, mild red pasilla or ancho chiles; or 1
    can (7 oz.) California green chiles, seeded
    Water
½ cup olive oil or salad oil
¼ cup wine vinegar
2 tablespoons firmly packed brown sugar
5 *each* whole black peppers and whole cloves
2 bay leaves
4 cups (about 1 lb.) grated dry jack or Parmesan
    cheese
16 slices French bread
    Paprika

Wash red chiles, if used, and place in a pan with 1/2 inch water; cover and simmer gently for about 5 min-

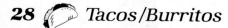

28 *Tacos/Burritos*

utes. Pull out seeds under running water. Drain and dry chiles on paper toweling.

Place red or green chiles in shallow baking dish. Mix together oil, vinegar, brown sugar, black peppers, cloves, and bay leaves; pour over chiles. Cover; let stand for about 8 hours or until next day at room temperature.

Remove and drain chiles; cut in half and set aside. Discard black peppers, cloves, and bay leaves; stir oil mixture into grated cheese. To assemble, cover each slice of French bread with chile half, about 1/3-inch layer of cheese mixture, and a sprinkling of paprika; serve. Makes 16 sandwiches.

Tortillas with Cheese

Quesadillas (keh-sah-*thee*-yas)

Mexican cooks have lots of ways of stuffing a tortilla. This quick and easy one resembles our grilled cheese sandwich.

A good melting cheese is basic to all fillings for quesadillas, but any other addition is at the discretion of the cook. Typically they are seasoned with chiles and onion; some also contain meat.

Our version uses flour tortillas; instead of frying, we broiled them to melt the cheese and crisp the tortillas.

¼ cup *each* **shredded Cheddar and jack cheese**
1 sliced mild onion, separated into rings (optional)
1 tablespoon chopped, seeded, canned California green chile (optional)
1 flour tortilla (page 74 or purchased)
    About 2 teaspoons grated Parmesan cheese
    About 2 teaspoons melted butter or margarine

Distribute Cheddar, jack, onion, and chile, if desired, over half the tortilla to within 1/2 inch of edge; sprinkle

with Parmesan. Fold tortilla over and brush both sides with butter. Broil about 3 inches from heat until top is lightly browned (about 2 minutes). Turn over and broil until other side is browned and cheese is melted (about 2 more minutes). Serve immediately. Makes 1 quesadilla.

To make spicier quesadillas, drizzle 1 tablespoon taco sauce over filling.

To substitute a different cheese, pick one that melts easily, such as Swiss, American, or teleme.

To make a meat filling, omit either Cheddar or jack; add 1 slice or about 1/4 cup diced cooked chicken, turkey, ham, or beef.

Picadillo Turnovers

Empanadas de Picadillo
(em-pah-*nah*-thas deh pee-kah-*thee*-yoh)

These turnovers filled with meat, fruit, and nuts are frequently served as between meal snacks. You can make them almost any size, to serve as an entrée, snack, or hors d'oeuvres—miniature ones are called empanaditas (little turnovers).

1 teaspoon butter or margarine
½ pound *each* **lean ground beef and lean ground pork (or 1 lb. ground beef)**
1 large clove garlic, minced or pressed
½ cup *each* **tomato purée and seedless raisins**
¼ cup dry sherry
2 teaspoons ground cinnamon
1 teaspoon salt
½ teaspoon ground cloves
2 tablespoons vinegar
1 tablespoon sugar
¾ cup (¼ lb.) slivered almonds
    Pastry for double-crust 9-inch pie
    Salad oil (optional)

In a wide frying pan, melt butter over medium heat; add meat and cook, stirring often, until meat loses pinkness. Drain off excess fat. Stir in garlic, tomato purée, raisins, sherry, cinnamon, salt, cloves, vinegar, and sugar. Cook, uncovered, over medium heat for 20 minutes or until most of the liquid has evaporated. Add almonds; cool.

Prepare pastry using your favorite recipe or a packaged mix. Roll out to 1/8-inch thickness and cut out 3-inch circles for little turnovers, 4 or 5-inch circles for large turnovers. Spoon filling mixture evenly on one side of each pastry round, moisten edges of pastry, fold over, and seal.

Heat at least 1 inch of oil to 370° and cook turnovers until brown on both sides; or bake in a 400° oven for 15 to 20 minutes or until brown. Makes 3½ dozen small or about 15 large turnovers.

Main-dish Specialties

Chiles rellenos to paella

In the United States, nearly every Mexican restaurant offers tacos, tostadas, tamales, enchiladas, and chiles rellenos. But in Mexico, the menu might also include a variety of broiled or roasted meats and poultry— usually very simply seasoned. Carne asada, Jalisco-style beefsteak, and barbecued flank steak sandwiches are delicious examples of the Mexicans' straightforward approach to cooking beef.

Poultry, seafood, and eggs are popular entrées, too. They are the foundation of such Mexican classics as chicken or turkey mole, chicken with rice, paella, and huevos rancheros. All can be easily duplicated at home with a styling and quality suitable for entertaining.

Less dramatic, but packed with slow-simmered flavor, are a number of stew-type dishes you can enjoy as is or enclose in a tortilla, burrito-style, to eat out of hand. Chile verde and pork stews are typical choices.

At serving time, these main-dish specialties are usually accompanied by rice, beans, and heated tortillas.

Carne Asada Supper

Cena de Carne Asada
(*seh*-nah deh *kar*-neh ah-*sah*-thah)

Carne asada in Spanish means "roasted or barbecued meat," but in some parts of Mexico it is also the name given to a particular dish. There are nearly as many versions of this dish as there are cooks, but one common characteristic is the way the meat is sliced. Beef or pork, usually the tenderloin, is cut in thin strips at a sharp diagonal to the grain of the meat.

Beef skirt steaks are exceptionally flavorful and tender prepared in this manner; however, you will probably have to order them ahead. Be sure to direct your butcher to trim off the fat but not to roll or tenderize the steaks. Flank steak can be used as a substitute. Then allow 6 minutes to a side on the grill for rare meat; slice across grain. (See photograph at left.)

⅓ cup *each* wine vinegar and olive oil
1 teaspoon oregano leaves, crumbled
½ teaspoon coarsely ground pepper
3 to 3½ pounds skirt steak, well trimmed of fat
   but neither rolled nor tenderized
Salsa fresca (recipe follows)

Combine vinegar and olive oil, oregano, and pepper. Place skirt steaks in a deep bowl and pour in the vinegar marinade; mix well. Let stand at room temperature for at least an hour; turn meat occasionally.

Lift steaks from marinade and place 4 or 5 inches above a solid bed of medium-glowing coals. Grill for 4 or 5 minutes on a side for rare meat; cut in serving pieces and accompany with salsa fresca. Makes 6 to 8 servings.

Salsa fresca. Peel and seed 4 medium-size **tomatoes** and cut in large chunks; set aside. Just before cooking carne asada, set a shallow pan on grill and melt 2 tablespoons **butter** or margarine. Then add 1 finely

 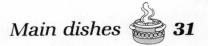

chopped large **onion** and 1/2 **green pepper,** seeded and chopped. Cook on grill, stirring, until onion is soft. Push to a cool area of grill. When steaks have cooked for about 3 minutes, add tomato chunks to onion and stir just to heat through. Season with **salt** and **pepper**, and serve salsa to spoon onto portions of meat.

Carne Asada Barbecue

Carne Asada (*kar*-neh ah-*sah*-thah)

Another version of carne asada uses mild sausage with beef and pork tenderloin. Here the meat is cooked quickly over very hot coals, at the table if outdoors. Use a Mexican clay brasero, Japanese hibachi, or other small barbecue. You need a solid bed of hot glowing coals (8 to 16 briquets) 1 to 2 inches below the grill.

> 6 mild chorizo, 2 to 3 oz. *each*
> Water
> 1½ to 1¾ pounds beef tenderloin, trimmed of fat
> 1 pork tenderloin (about ¾ lb.), trimmed of fat
> Coarse (kosher) salt or regular salt
> Sautéed green peppers (page 68)
> Fried bananas (page 68)

Cover chorizo with water, bring to a boil, reduce heat, and simmer, covered, for 20 minutes. Drain and let cool.

Cut beef and pork into diagonal slices about 1/4 inch thick and arrange separately on a large tray along with chorizo. Cook sausage and slices of meat on a grill 1 or 2 inches above a solid bed of very hot coals. Cook pork until it loses most of the pink color, then

turn to cook evenly until all pinkness is gone. Cook beef to the degree of doneness you desire. Cook sausage just until lightly browned and heated through.

Sprinkle coarse salt onto beef and pork before eating. Accompany with sautéed green peppers and fried bananas. Makes 6 servings.

Beefsteak, Jalisco-style

Bistec de Jalisco (*bees*-tec deh ha-*lees*-koh)

Barbecued steak, enhanced with a generous flavoring of fresh orange juice, is typical of the simple yet delicious entrées found in the state of Jalisco in western Mexico.

> About 3 pounds top round steak, cut 2 inches thick
> Pepper
> 1 large orange
> Salt

Trim off all fat and make diagonal 3/8-inch-deep cuts in surface of steak about 1 inch apart. Rub meat lightly with pepper. Grill about 5 to 6 inches above a solid bed of medium-hot coals for about 10 minutes on a side for rare meat or cook to degree of doneness you prefer.

Transfer meat to carving board and squeeze juice of orange evenly over meat. Sprinkle lightly with salt. Cut meat in thin, slanting slices and moisten each piece with accumulated drippings. Makes 8 to 10 servings.

Barbecued Sandwiches

Sandwiches a la Barbacoa
(*sahn*-wee-ches ah lah bar-ba-*ko*-ah)

This picnic idea calls for rolling up flour tortillas with flank steak strips and tomato salsa inside to make sandwiches.

Plan to marinate the meat in advance and carry it to your picnic site, along with premixed salsa, avocado, flour tortillas, and any materials you need for barbecuing. Buy the largest flour tortillas available; in a Mexican delicatessen you may find the extra-large (about 10-inch) size.

> ¼ cup *each* olive oil and white wine vinegar
> ½ teaspoon *each* salt and oregano leaves, crumbled
> ⅛ teaspoon pepper
> 3 cloves garlic, minced or pressed
> 1 large flank steak (about 1½ lb.)
> 12 flour tortillas (page 74 or purchased)
> Tomato salsa (recipe follows)

 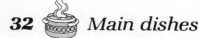

In a 7 by 11-inch baking dish, mix together olive oil, vinegar, salt, oregano, pepper, and garlic. Add steak, cover, and refrigerate for at least 6 hours or until next day; during that time, turn steak over several times.

When ready to cook, place steak on barbecue grill about 4 inches above a solid bed of evenly ignited charcoal briquets. Allow 5 to 8 minutes on each side for rare meat. Remove from grill and slice across grain into thin strips.

Meanwhile, heat tortillas by placing one at a time directly on grill, turning once, until soft and hot (about 30 seconds on a side). Stack tortillas and keep warm by wrapping in dampened cloth or in foil.

Serve sliced meat in warmed tortillas with salsa to spoon over. Makes about 6 servings of 2 sandwiches each.

Tomato salsa. Peel, seed, and finely chop 2 medium-size **tomatoes.** Turn into a bowl and stir in 3 **green onions** (finely chopped), 2 tablespoons seeded and chopped canned **California green chiles,** 2 tablespoons chopped fresh **coriander** (cilantro), 1/2 teaspoon **salt,** and 1 tablespoon **olive oil.** Cover and chill. Just before serving, peel and dice 1 **avocado** and gently mix in.

Beef Tongue in Chipotle Sauce

Lengua de Res con Salsa de Chipotle
(*len*-guah deh rres kon *sahl*-sah deh chi-*pot*-le)

The smoky, pungent flavor of pickled chipotle peppers distinguishes this dish. Imported from Mexico, they are plump, brick-red peppers canned in a rich, red sauce. Look for them in Mexican markets or use the suggested substitute. Because they are hot, start with half a can and add more if desired.

    3-pound beef tongue (smoked, corned,
        or fresh)
    Water
    2 large onions, sliced
    2 cloves garlic, minced or pressed
    2 tablespoons salad oil
    1 can (1 lb. 12 oz.) tomatoes
    ½ teaspoon *each* ground cumin, salt, and pepper
    ½ to 1 can (6½ to 7 oz.) pickled chipotle peppers
        (or substitute 1½ to 2 tablespoons firmly
        packed brown sugar, ¼ cup white vinegar, 1
        teaspoon *each* paprika and sesame seed oil,
        1 to 1½ teaspoons crushed red pepper, ½
        teaspoon hickory flavored salt, and ¼
        teaspoon bottled liquid smoke)
    1 large green bell pepper, seeded and cut into
        thin rings

In a 5-quart kettle, place well scrubbed beef tongue. Cover with water, bring to a boil, and cook, covered, for 3 hours over low heat or until fork tender. Remove from pan and cool. Remove skin; trim off bone, roots, and excess fat. Slice tongue thinly.

Meanwhile, in a wide frying pan over medium heat, cook onions and garlic in oil, stirring, until golden.

In a blender jar, combine tomatoes and their liquid, cumin, salt, pepper, pickled chipotle peppers and their sauce. Whirl until smooth. Add to onions and garlic; bring to simmer. Stir in sliced tongue, cover, and simmer for about 25 minutes or until heated through. Garnish with green pepper rings. Makes 6 to 8 servings.

Tongue & Vegetables

Salpicon (sahl-pee-*kohn*)

Salpicon translates into English as "salmagundi," or—if you need help on that word—a salad-like dish featuring meat with vegetables and dressing. Start this supper salad a day ahead so the cooked meat and vegetables can chill.

Complete the menu with warm, soft corn tortillas and butter, cold Mexican beer or orange juice, and caramel custard (page 82).

    2½ to 3-pound beef tongue (smoked or fresh)
    2 quarts water
    1 *each* carrot, onion, and celery stalk, sliced
    ¼ cup white wine vinegar
    1 teaspoon salt
    ½ teaspoon whole black pepper
    1 teaspoon oregano leaves
    ¼ teaspoon cumin seed
    Tongue marinade (directions follow)
    Cooked vegetables (directions follow)
    Shredded lettuce and a few leaves
    Parsley and sliced mild onion rings

Scrub tongue well under running water, then place in a 5-quart kettle. Add water, carrot, onion, celery, vinegar, salt, pepper, oregano, and cumin. Cover and bring to boiling, then reduce heat to simmer and cook for 2½ to 3 hours or until meat is fork tender. Let cool in broth.

Remove tongue, reserving liquid; skin tongue, trimming away any fat and bones. Slice tongue thinly and place in a deep bowl. Pour tongue marinade over meat and chill, covered, overnight.

Meanwhile, pour tongue broth through wire strainer; discard residue. Skim fat from broth (or chill and lift off fat); use as cooking liquid for vegetables.

To serve, cover a large rimmed platter with shredded lettuce and arrange tongue and cooked vegetables on top. Pour over tongue marinade and enough vegetable marinade to moisten salad lightly. Decorate platter with lettuce leaves and parsley, and garnish meat with onion rings. Makes 6 servings.

(Continued on next page)

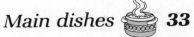

Tongue marinade. Blend together 1 finely chopped mild **onion**, 3/4 cup **olive oil**, 1/2 cup **white wine vinegar**, 1/2 teaspoon **salt**, 1/4 teaspoon **pepper**, and 1 teaspoon **oregano** leaves.

Cooked vegetables. In a large pan, bring reserved **tongue broth** to boiling. Add 6 whole medium-size **carrots** and 6 medium-size **turnips**. Cover and boil gently 15 to 20 minutes or until fork tender. Remove vegetables from liquid with a slotted spoon and set aside.

Meanwhile, cut 3 large boiling **potatoes** in quarters and trim sections round to resemble small whole potatoes. Cook potatoes, covered, in boiling broth just until barely tender when pierced. Remove pan from heat; return carrots and turnips to liquid, adding 1/3 cup **olive oil** and 2 tablespoons **vinegar**. Chill, covered, overnight. If stock gels, warm slightly to release vegetables.

Meanwhile, in a large pan, cook, covered, 3 or 4 medium-size **zucchini** (each cut in half lengthwise) in boiling **salted water** to cover for 10 minutes or until fork tender. Drain and chill quickly in **ice water**, drain well again. Moisten zucchini lightly with **olive oil** (or salad oil) and chill, covered. Drain vegetables before arranging with meat.

Let guests fill their own burritos, folding flour tortillas around a filling of braised pork with red or green chile sauce (recipes below). For a stunning centerpiece, fresh fruit platter with jicama slices and Oaxacan peanuts (page 9).

Trim and discard fat from meat and cut into 1-inch cubes. In a wide frying pan, heat oil over medium-high heat; add meat a few pieces at a time and cook until lightly brown. Push to sides of pan, add onion, garlic, chili powder, cumin, and oregano; cook until onion is limp. Stir in water, sugar, salt, and tomato paste; simmer, covered, until pork is fork tender (about 1 hour). Skim off fat and discard. Stir in cream and cook, stirring, until mixture boils.

Turn into a serving dish and garnish with pumpkin seeds. To serve, fill warm tortillas with meat and garnish with avocado, tomato, and sour cream. Offer lime to squeeze over servings. Makes 6 servings.

Braised Pork with Red Chile Sauce

Puerco Perdigado con Salsa de Chile Rojo
(*puer*-koh per-thi-*gah*-tho kohn *sahl*-sah deh *chee*-leh *ro*-hoh)

Chili powder flavors the red sauce of this entrée. Serve with rice or use it to fill warm, soft, flour tortillas for a burrito, along with accompaniments of avocado and tomato wedges. (See photograph at right.)

- 3 pounds lean boneless pork butt
- 2 tablespoons salad oil
- 2 large onions, chopped
- 2 cloves garlic, minced or pressed
- 5 to 6 teaspoons chili powder
- 1 teaspoon ground cumin
- 1½ teaspoons oregano leaves, crumbled
- 1¼ cups water
- 1 teaspoon sugar
- 1½ teaspoons salt
- 3 tablespoons canned tomato paste
- ½ cup whipping cream
  Roasted pumpkin seeds (page 9)
  Warm, soft flour tortillas (page 74 or purchased) or hot cooked rice
  Garnishes: 1 large avocado, peeled, pitted, and sliced; 1 large tomato, cut in wedges; sour cream sprinkled with chili powder
- 2 limes, cut in wedges

Braised Pork with Green Chile Sauce

Puerco Perdigado con Salsa de Chile Verde
(*puer*-koh per-thi-*gah*-tho kohn *sahl*-sah deh *chee*-leh *ver*-deh)

Mild canned California green chiles season this meaty pork stew. Serve it with rice or as a burrito filling. For burritos, spoon pork mixture into warm, soft flour tortillas, add sour cream, tomato wedges, and a squeeze of lime juice, and fold to enclose.

- 3 pounds lean boneless pork butt
- 2 tablespoons salad oil
- 1 large onion, chopped
- 2 cloves garlic, minced or pressed
- 2 large green bell peppers, seeded and chopped
- 1 large can (7 oz.) California green chiles, seeded and chopped
- 1 teaspoon oregano leaves, crumbled
- ½ teaspoon ground cumin
- 1½ teaspoons salt
- ½ cup chopped fresh coriander (cilantro) or 2 tablespoons dried cilantro
- 1 tablespoon wine vinegar
- ¼ cup water
- 1 large or 2 medium-size tomatoes, cut in wedges
  Hot cooked rice or warm, soft, flour tortillas (page 74 or purchased)
- 1 cup sour cream
- 2 limes, cut in wedges

(Continued on page 36)

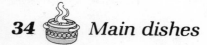

Trim and discard fat and cut pork in 1-inch cubes. In a wide frying pan, heat oil over medium-high heat; add meat a few pieces at a time and cook until lightly browned. Push meat to sides of pan and add onion, garlic, and bell peppers; sauté until limp. Stir in chiles, oregano, cumin, salt, coriander, vinegar, and water; cover and simmer until meat is fork tender (about 1 hour). Skim off fat and discard.

Spoon into serving dish and garnish with tomato wedges. Serve with hot cooked rice; have guests spoon sour cream and squeeze lime juice onto servings. Makes 6 servings.

To barbecue, bank about 20 low-glowing coals on each side of fire grill. Place a drip pan in center. Place meat on greased cooking grill about 6 inches above pan.

Cover barbecue and adjust dampers or drape a large piece of heavy-duty foil over meat. Cook for about 2 hours or until meat thermometer inserted in thickest portion registers 140° for slightly pink meat; or cook until done to your liking. After about 1 hour, add 6 to 8 briquets to each side.

Let roast stand in a warm place for about 20 minutes, then garnish with parsley and radishes. Slice meat thinly to serve. Accompany with meat juices. Makes 6 to 8 servings.

Leg of Lamb, Yucatan-style

Pierna de Cordero Asado, estilo Yucateco
(pee-*er*-na deh kor-*the*-ro ah-*sah*-tho yoo-ka-*tan*)

The unusual tropical spice, achiote (ah-*show*-tey)— available occasionally in Mexican markets—is the authentic seasoning for this leg of lamb. Achiote is used extensively in Yucatan and Central America principally for the rich red color and mild, delicate flavor it gives to foods. You can achieve a similar but less colorful effect with cinnamon and chili powder.

Have your butcher bone and butterfly a leg of lamb. Rub the achiote or cinnamon-chili powder mixture over meat. Make citrus-cornbread stuffing (use home-baked or frozen cornbread or muffins) and pat thinly over the cut side of the lamb. Then reshape meat to make a compact roast for barbecuing.

  1 tablespoon whole achiote (see above) or ½
    teaspoon chili powder and ⅛ teaspoon
    ground cinnamon
  ½ teaspoon coarsely ground pepper
  1½ teaspoons salt
  2 tablespoons salad oil
    About 6-pound leg of lamb, boned and
    butterflied
  1 tablespoon grated orange peel
  3 tablespoons orange juice
  ½ teaspoon grated lemon peel
  ½ cup packed cornbread or corn muffin crumbs
  1 tablespoon minced onion
    Parsley and radishes

Crush achiote by whirling to a powder in a blender (or grind achiote through a pepper mill set at medium grind). Blend achiote (or chili and cinnamon) with pepper, salt, and salad oil. Rub over all surfaces of lamb.

Blend thoroughly orange peel, orange juice, lemon peel, cornbread crumbs, and onion. Spread mixture over inside of lamb, then reshape leg into a compact form and skewer or tie with heavy thread to hold.

Sesame Seed Chicken

Pipian (pee-pee-*an*)

Lightly toasted sesame seed, pumpkin seeds, and spices give surprisingly heavy body to this light brown-colored sauce. The flavor is decidedly peanutlike.

Pipian comes from the pre-Columbian cultures and is sometimes described as Indian fricassee. We do not cook the meat in the sauce, however, since pipian behaves rather curiously. The seeds, whirled smooth with broth, make a thin liquid that, when heated, thickens considerably and becomes grainy. Mexican cooks partially control this with a high proportion of fat. For American tastes, we recommend whirling the heated sauce to smoothness once again, then warming it very gently to spoon over the hot chicken.

  3 tablespoons sesame seed
  ½ cup plain or salted pumpkin seeds (shelled)
  1 small clove garlic
  2 tablespoons salad oil
  ¼ teaspoon ground cinnamon
  ⅛ teaspoon ground cloves
  ¾ teaspoon chili powder
  ¾ cup regular-strength chicken broth
    Salt
  1½ tablespoons lime juice
  2 hot, whole, boned, cooked chicken breasts
    (split), or 4 hot cooked chicken legs with
    thighs attached
    Shredded lettuce
    Sliced green onions and lime wedges

In a pan, combine sesame seed, pumpkin seeds, garlic, and salad oil. Stir over medium heat until sesame seed turns a pale golden brown. Remove at once from heat and stir in cinnamon, cloves, and chili powder. In a blender, whirl mixture until smooth, adding broth a little at a time. Add salt to taste.

Heat sauce over medium heat, stirring, until it be-

 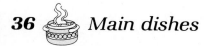

gins to bubble and thicken. Return to blender and whirl until smooth. You can cover sauce and refrigerate several days.

To serve, very gently heat sauce with lime juice, stirring constantly, just until hot to touch. Spoon over hot chicken. Surround with lettuce and garnish with onion and lime wedges. Squeeze lime over to taste. Makes 4 servings.

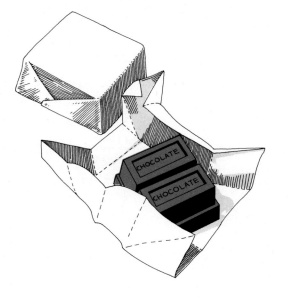

Pork Stew with Tomatillos

Cocido de Puerco con Tomatillos
(coh-*see*-doh deh *puer*-koh kohn toh-mah-*tee*-yos)

Tomatillos are Mexico's tasty, tart, green tomatoes. Canned tomatillos are widely available in Mexican food sections of our supermarkets. They add piquancy to this stew.

    2½ pounds lean boneless pork butt
    2 tablespoons salad oil
    1 large onion, chopped
    2 cloves garlic, minced or pressed
    1½ cups chopped tomatillos, fresh or canned
        (drained)
    1 can (7 oz.) California green chiles, seeded and
        chopped
    1 teaspoon marjoram leaves
    1 teaspoon salt
    ¼ cup lightly packed chopped fresh coriander
        (cilantro) or 1 tablespoon dried cilantro
    ½ cup water
        Fresh coriander leaves (cilantro) or fresh
        tomatillo wedges
        Hot cooked rice
    1 cup sour cream

Trim and discard fat and cut pork in 1-inch cubes. In a wide frying pan, heat salad oil over medium-high heat; add meat a few pieces at a time and cook until lightly browned. Push meat to sides of pan and add onion; cook until onion is limp.

Stir in garlic, tomatillos, chiles, marjoram, salt, coriander, and water. Cover and simmer until meat is fork tender (about 1 hour). Skim off fat.

Spoon into serving dish and garnish with coriander leaves. Serve with hot cooked rice and pass sour cream to spoon over servings. Makes 4 to 6 servings.

Chicken Mole

Mole de Pollo (*moh*-leh deh *poh*-yoh)

Rich chocolate distinguishes this national dish of Mexico. Cook chicken and sauce a day ahead, if desired. Chicken can be served in whole pieces or boned, skinned, and cut in chunks. Serve with fresh cooked vegetables and rice.(See photograph, page 38.)

    2 broiler-fryer chickens (about 3 lb. *each*), cut in
        pieces
    1 large onion, sliced
    3 whole cloves garlic
    1 can (about 14 oz.) regular-strength chicken
        broth
        Mole sauce (recipe follows)
    2 tablespoons chopped fresh coriander
        (cilantro)
    4 to 6 cups hot cooked rice
        Fresh vegetable condiments (page 39)

Place all chicken but breasts (reserve giblets for other uses) in a 5-quart kettle. Add onion, garlic, and chicken broth. Cover and simmer for 25 minutes. Cut whole breasts in half and add to kettle; continue to simmer, covered, for 20 minutes or until thigh meat is no longer pink near bone when slashed.

Lift chicken from broth, set aside to cool slightly; leave whole or pull off and discard skin and bone. Cut each breast into 3 pieces; cut other large pieces into same size as breast meat pieces, if desired.

Pour broth through a wire strainer and reserve; discard vegetables. Skim off fat and discard. Measure broth; if less than 3 cups, add water; if more than 3 cups, boil to reduce. If made ahead, cover and chill chicken and broth separately.

Heat mole sauce to simmering. Add chicken and simmer until meat is hot. Transfer meat to serving dish and sprinkle with coriander. Pour remaining sauce into a bowl. Serve meat and sauce over hot cooked rice; accompany with vegetables. Makes 6 servings.

Mole sauce. In a blender, whirl until smooth 2 tablespoons **chili powder,** 20 whole blanched **almonds,**

(Continued on page 39)

 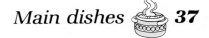

Center your own fiesta around chicken mole (page 37). Guests add garnishes from little dishes grouped around main dish. Guacamole for tortilla chips (page 9), refreshing orange salad (page 18), and crusty hard rolls (page 77) are traditional touches. And for dessert, hot baked pineapple in shell (page 84).

. . . Chicken Mole (cont'd.)

1/4 cup diced green tipped **banana,** 1 teaspoon *each* ground **cinnamon** and **salt,** 2 **corn tortillas** (torn in pieces), 2 tablespoons **sesame seed,** 1 tablespoon **pine nuts,** and enough reserved **chicken broth** (see preceding directions) to blend smoothly. Pour sauce into pan; add remaining broth, 6 tablespoons **butter** or margarine, and 1 ounce **semisweet chocolate.** Heat to simmering over medium heat, stirring. (If made ahead, cover and refrigerate as long as 1 week; then reheat.)

Fresh vegetable condiments. Place each of the following in individual small dishes (cover and chill if done ahead): 4 medium-size **tomatoes,** chopped; 1 bunch (about 1 cup) fresh **coriander** (cilantro) or parsley; 4 **green onions,** thinly sliced; 1½ cups thinly sliced **radishes** (about 1 bunch); 1/3 cup seeded and chopped canned **California green chiles;** 3 **limes,** cut into wedges; and 1/4 cup **sesame seed.**

Turkey in Mole Sauce

Mole Poblano de Guajolote
(*moh*-leh po-*blan*-noh deh guah-ho-*lo*-teh)

Another popular mole variation uses leftover cooked turkey. Spoon chunks of mole into warm tortillas. Embellish with guacamole, and eat out of hand.

> Mole sauce (page 37)
> 3 cans (about 14 oz. *each*) regular-strength chicken broth
> 6 cups cooked turkey or chicken, boned and skinned and cut into ½ by 2-inch pieces
> Salt
> ¼ cup chopped fresh coriander (cilantro)
> 18 flour or corn tortillas (page 74 or purchased)
> Guacamole (page 9 or purchased)

Prepare mole sauce using canned chicken broth.

Combine mole sauce and turkey in a wide frying pan set over medium heat; cook, uncovered, until sauce is hot and thick. Add salt to taste, then transfer to a serving dish; top with coriander.

Follow directions for reheating tortillas (page 76).

To serve, let diners spoon chunks of turkey mole mixture into warm tortillas, embellish with a spoonful of guacamole, fold, and eat out of hand. Makes 6 to 9 servings.

Green Mole

Mole Verde (moh-leh *ver*-deh)

Mole verde, a dish of meat with "green mole" sauce, gets its characteristic flavor and green color from the tomatillo, a walnut-size, tart green tomato sold fresh or in cans. This recipe uses the more available canned tomatillos.

> About 2 pounds sliced cooked turkey, chicken, or pork
> 2½ cups green tomatillo sauce (page 63)
> Salt
> Small lettuce leaves
> Purchased mild pickled chiles (optional)
> About 1 cup sour cream

Arrange meat (cut as thin as you like) in a wide frying pan; pour tomato sauce over all. Cover and warm over low heat; when mixture begins to bubble slightly, simmer for 5 to 10 minutes. Add salt to taste.

Arrange meat with sauce on rimmed platter. Garnish with lettuce leaves and pickled chiles, if desired; serve with sour cream. Makes 4 to 6 servings.

Chilaquiles in Casserole

Chilaquiles (chee-lah-*kee*-les)

The various ingredients for this main dish can be prepared the day before. Assemble the casserole no more than 4 hours before cooking time to keep tortillas crisp. Serve with green salad.

> 12 corn tortillas (page 74 or purchased) cut in strips and fried (page 77) or 6 cups purchased tortilla chips
> 2 cups refried beans (page 68 or canned)
> 3 cups cooked and diced ham
> 3 cups cooked and diced chicken or turkey
> Tomato sauce (recipe follows)
> 3 cups (about 12 oz.) mild Cheddar cheese, shredded
> Minced parsley and pitted ripe olives

Distribute half the tortilla strips over bottom of a shallow 3-quart casserole (about 9 by 13 inches). Spoon beans in dollops evenly over tortillas. Mix ham and chicken and spoon half the mixture over beans, then pour half the tomato sauce over meat and top with half the cheese. Repeat layers of tortillas, meat, tomato sauce, and cover with remaining cheese. (At this point you can cover and chill casserole for as long as 4 hours.)

Bake, uncovered, in a 375° oven for 30 minutes (if refrigerated, 45 minutes). Garnish with parsley and olives and serve hot. Makes 8 to 10 servings.

(Continued on next page)

 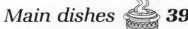

Tomato sauce. In a wide frying pan, cook 1 cup chopped **onion** and 2 cloves **garlic**, minced or pressed, in 2 tablespoons **olive oil** or salad oil, stirring, until vegetables are limp. Pour in 1 large can (1 lb. 12 oz.) **tomatoes** and their liquid; break up tomatoes with a spoon. Add 1 cup regular-strength **chicken broth**, 1 can (6 oz.) **tomato paste**, 1 tablespoon **chili powder**, and 1/2 teaspoon *each* **salt** and ground **cumin**. Simmer, uncovered, until reduced to 3 cups, stirring occasionally.

Blend 2 teaspoons **cornstarch** to a smooth paste with 1 tablespoon **water** and blend with 2 cups (1 pt.) **sour cream**. Blend some tomato sauce with sour cream, then return all to tomato sauce; bring to a boil, stirring. Remove from heat. Remove seeds and pith from about 2 cans (4 oz. *each*) whole **California green chiles**; coarsely chop. Add chiles to sauce, a portion at a time, tasting until flavor is pleasantly hot. Chill.

Rice & Sausage

Arroz con Chorizo (ah-*rrros* kohn choh-*ree*-soh)

Avocado and egg slices garnish this colorful main-dish casserole.

    1 pound chorizo (purchased), skinned, or 2
        cups bulk chorizo (page 64)
      Salad oil
    2 cups rice
    ¼ cup minced onion
    ⅓ cup tomato purée
    2 cups peas
      About 4 cups regular-strength beef or chicken
        broth
      Salt
    2 hard-cooked eggs, sliced
    1 large avocado, sliced

In a wide frying pan over medium-high heat, cook chorizo until browned, breaking apart as it cooks, adding oil if necessary. Mash with a fork; set aside. Brown rice and onion in drippings, then discard any remaining drippings. Add chorizo, tomato purée, peas, and broth. Cover and cook over medium heat for 25 minutes (or in a 350° oven for about 50 minutes) or until rice is tender to bite. Add more broth if needed; add salt to taste. Just before serving, garnish with slices of egg and avocado. Makes 4 to 6 servings.

Paella

(pah-*ay*-yah)
Spanish Seafood and Rice

Paella, a seafood classic, is one of Spain's contributions to the cuisine of Mexico. This dish includes rice and usually both meat and seafood. But other ingredients used in paella vary from region to region in Mexico and even from one family to another.

An authentic paella pan is large, round or oval, and shallow, with a small handle on each side. A large heavy pan, such as a Dutch oven, works satisfactorily. Serve paella in wide-rimmed soup bowls.

    1 pound lean pork spareribs, cut apart
      Olive oil
    ¾ pound chorizo (purchased), skinned, or 1½
        cups bulk chorizo (page 64)
    2 cloves garlic, minced or pressed
    3 large tomatoes, peeled and cut into wedges
    6 cups water
    1 teaspoon salt
    ¼ teaspoon pepper
    1 to 2 dozen small clams (or mussels) in shells
    1 to 1½ pounds shellfish (shrimp, langostinos,
        lobster tails, or crayfish)
    2 cups rice
    1 can (4 oz.) pimentos, drained and sliced
    1 cup fresh or thawed frozen peas
    ¼ cup chopped parsley

In a wide frying pan over medium heat, cook spareribs until brown on all sides; add oil if needed. Add chorizo to pan and brown well, breaking meat apart as it cooks. Discard drippings. Add garlic, tomatoes, water, salt, and pepper. Simmer, uncovered, for 20 minutes.

Meanwhile, scrub clams or mussels well to remove all sand and barnacles. Shell and devein shrimp; cut lobster tails into 1-inch sections; or drop crayfish into boiling water to cover for about 5 minutes or until bright pink (use tails only).

Slowly add rice to simmering mixture. Cook, covered, over low heat for about 20 minutes, stirring occasionally; skim off accumulated fat. Add clams, shellfish, pimentos, peas, and parsley; cover and cook for about 10 minutes longer or until the rice is tender to bite and clams have popped open. Serve immediately. Makes 6 to 8 servings.

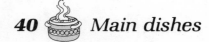

Macaroni & Sausage

Macarron con Chorizo
(mah-kah-*rrron* kohn choh-*ree*-soh)

The spices in the chorizo sausage are the main flavoring in this hearty dish.

- 1 pound large tube-shaped macaroni
  Boiling salted water
- 1 pound chorizo (purchased), skinned, or 2 cups bulk chorizo (page 64)
  Salad oil
- ½ cup minced onion
- 3 cans (8 oz. *each*) tomato sauce
- 2 tablespoons chopped fresh coriander (cilantro) or 1 teaspoon oregano leaves, crumbled
  Salt and pepper
- 1½ cups (about 6 oz.) jack cheese, shredded

In a 5-quart kettle, cook macaroni in a generous amount of boiling salted water until just tender to bite; drain.

In a wide frying pan, cook chorizo until browned, adding oil if needed. Break meat apart as it cooks. Remove meat and set aside.

In pan drippings, cook onion until soft; discard remaining drippings. Add tomato sauce, coriander, salt and pepper to taste. Arrange in a greased 3-quart shallow baking dish in layers: macaroni, chorizo, and sauce. Top with cheese. Bake, uncovered, in a 350° oven for about 30 minutes or until bubbly and hot throughout. Makes 6 servings.

Chicken with Rice

Arroz con Pollo (ah-*rrros* kohn *poh*-yoh)

Tomatoes plus a garnish of peas or asparagus tips give lots of color to this rice dish. All the ingredients cook together in chicken stock until the rice has absorbed the liquid.

- ½ pound diced salt pork
- 2 tablespoons olive oil or salad oil
- 3 to 3½-pound broiler-fryer chicken, cut up
- ½ cup chopped onion
- 1 clove garlic, minced or pressed
- 2 large peeled tomatoes (or 1 cup drained canned tomatoes), cut in chunks
- 1 cup rice
  About 2 cups regular-strength chicken broth
  Salt and pepper
- 1 package (10 oz.) frozen peas or asparagus tips

In a wide frying pan over medium heat, cook salt pork until well browned; set pork aside and discard drippings.

Add oil to pan and heat. Add chicken pieces and cook until well browned on all sides. Set chicken aside; discard all but 2 tablespoons of the drippings. Add onion and garlic and cook until onion is limp. Stir in tomatoes, rice, 2 cups of the broth, and browned pork. Return chicken to pan; cover and cook over low heat for about 45 minutes or until thigh meat is no longer pink when slashed and rice is tender to bite. (Add more broth if needed to prevent sticking.) Season to taste with salt and pepper.

Meanwhile, cook peas according to package directions. Arrange chicken and rice in a wide shallow serving dish; scatter cooked peas over top. Makes about 4 servings.

Chicken with Oranges

Pollo con Naranjas (*poh*-yoh kohn nah-*rahn*-has)

A most interesting combination of ingredients distinguishes this chicken dish—rich with spices, redolent with orange, and full of raisins, capers, and almonds.

- 3½-pound broiler-fryer chicken, cut in pieces
  Salt and pepper
- ⅛ teaspoon *each* ground cinnamon and ground cloves
- 3 tablespoons salad oil
- 2 cloves garlic, minced or pressed
- 1 medium-size onion, chopped
- 1 cup orange juice
  Ground saffron
- 2 tablespoons seedless raisins
- 1 tablespoon capers
- ½ cup coarsely chopped almonds
- 3 oranges, peeled and sliced

Sprinkle chicken with salt, pepper, cinnamon, and cloves. In a wide frying pan, heat oil over medium-high heat; add chicken and cook until well browned on all sides. Set aside. Discard all but 2 tablespoons drippings. Add garlic and onion to pan and cook until onion is limp. Return chicken and add orange juice, a pinch of saffron, raisins, and capers.

Cover and cook over low heat until chicken is no longer pink near bone when slashed (about 45 minutes). Stir in almonds just before serving. Garnish with orange slices. Makes 4 to 6 servings.

Fish & Rice Stew

Zarzuela (sahr-*sweh*-lah)

Seafood laden zarzuela goes together in a smooth sequence of steps. For a party, have all ingredients ready, then cook just before guests are due. Zarzuela can be kept up to 2 hours on an electric warming tray, but it's best if not reheated.

(Continued on next page)

 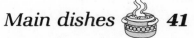

6 tablespoons olive oil or salad oil
3 large onions, finely chopped
1 cup minced parsley, lightly packed
2 cups rice
1 can (1 lb. 12 oz.) tomatoes
2 cans (8 oz. *each*) minced clams
2 bottles (8 oz. *each*) clam juice
2 cups water
¼ cup chopped fresh coriander (cilantro) or
  1 tablespoon dried cilantro leaves
2 to 2½ pounds boneless, skinned fish (such as
  Greenland turbot, halibut, lingcod, or sea
  bass) cut in 1½-inch chunks
½ pound scallops, cut in ½-inch chunks
  Salt and pepper
  Accompaniments (directions follow)

In a 5-quart kettle, combine oil and onions and place over medium-high heat; cook, stirring, until onion is soft. Stir in parsley and rice and continue cooking, stirring, until some of the rice is lightly toasted.

Stir in tomatoes and juices (break up tomatoes with a spoon), clams and their liquid, clam juice, water, and coriander. Bring to a boil, cover; reduce heat and simmer for 15 minutes.

Press fish chunks and scallops down into rice; continue to cook, covered, on low heat for about 10 minutes or until fish flakes readily when prodded in thickest portion with a fork and rice is tender to bite. Stir occasionally to prevent sticking and season to taste with salt and pepper.

Spoon mixture into a wide, shallow serving dish. Serve with accompaniments. Makes 10 to 12 servings.

Accompaniments. Mound 1/2 pound tiny, whole, cooked and shelled **shrimp** in the center of zarzuela. Peel, pit, and slice 1 or 2 large **avocados**; arrange around shrimp. Quarter 4 or 5 **limes;** squeeze some lime juice over avocado to prevent darkening. Place remaining limes in a dish. Put 2 cups **sour cream** in a dish. Sprinkle a few fresh **coriander** leaves (or chopped green onion) on shrimp and avocado. Squeeze lime and spoon sour cream onto each serving.

Baked Swordfish Manzanillo

Pez Espada al Horno a la Manzanillo
(pehs es-*pah*-than ahl *or*-noh man-sah-*nee*-yoh)

Quickly baked, firm-textured swordfish is generously coated with sliced green onions.

4 swordfish steaks (about 8 oz. *each*)
  Salt and pepper
4 to 6 tablespoons olive oil
½ cup sliced green onions, including some tops
  Garnishes: chopped parsley, tomato and lime
  wedges

Sprinkle swordfish steaks with salt and pepper. Place fish in a single layer in a baking dish; brush with olive oil, coating heavily. Sprinkle green onions over fish.

Bake, uncovered, in a 350° oven for about 20 minutes or until fish flakes easily when prodded with a fork. Remove to serving platter. Sprinkle with parsley and garnish with tomato and lime wedges. Makes 4 servings.

Bright pink shrimp on skewers are basted with garlic butter sauce while they cook (recipe below). To complement, puffy chile relleno casserole with marinara sauce served right from the oven (page 49).

Skewered Shrimp with Garlic Butter Sauce

Camaron a la Brocheta con Salsa de Mantequilla y Ajo (kah-mah-*ron* ah lah bro-*cheh*-tah kohn *sahl*-sah deh mahn-ten-*kee*-yay e *ah*-ho)

A dramatic presentation, skewered shrimp, broiled or barbecued until pink and juicy, are basted with garlic butter. Serve left over baste as a dipping sauce for the cooked shrimp. (See photograph at right.)

2 pounds medium-size shrimp
½ cup (¼ lb.) butter or margarine
½ cup olive oil
3 cloves garlic, minced or pressed
3 tablespoons minced parsley
2 tablespoons lemon juice

Peel and devein shrimp; to devein without cutting, slip a thin wooden skewer through back of each shrimp. Pull gently up through back, lifting and pulling out vein (if present, it can be seen). Repeat along back in several spots if vein breaks.

Impale 8 to 10 shrimp close together, on 2 parallel thin wooden skewers: put one skewer through thick section of shrimp, other through tail section to hold shrimp flat. Repeat with remaining shrimp.

Melt butter in a pan. Add oil, garlic, and parsley; heat just until bubbling, then remove sauce from heat.

Place skewered shrimp on a rack in a pan; brush generously with garlic sauce. Broil shrimp 4 inches from heat until they turn bright pink (about 4 minutes). Baste at least once with garlic sauce. Turn and broil on other side for about 3 minutes or until shrimp feel firm when pinched; baste once. (Or place skewers on a greased grill about 6 inches above a solid bed of low glowing coals. Cook and baste as directed for broiled shrimp.)

(Continued on page 44)

42 *Main dishes*

Arrange shrimp on a serving tray. Heat remaining garlic sauce to bubbling, add lemon juice, and pour into individual serving containers. Dip shrimps into garlic sauce to eat. Makes 4 to 6 servings.

Stuffed Chiles with Walnuts

Chiles en Nogada (*chee*-leh ehn noh-*gah*-tha)

A pink topping of pomegranate seeds adorns a mound of turkey under sour cream surrounded by split chiles.

1½ cups coarsely chopped walnuts
　　Boiling water
4 tablespoons butter or margarine
2 medium-size onions, finely chopped
3 tablespoons all-purpose flour
½ teaspoon *each* ground nutmeg and white
　　pepper
1 can (10½ oz.) condensed chicken broth
1 cup whipping cream or half-and-half (light
　　cream)
½ cup sour cream
　　Salt
2 cans (7 oz. *each*) whole California green chiles
6 cups cooked turkey or chicken, boned,
　　skinned, and cut in ½ by 2-inch pieces
1½ cups pomegranate seeds (about 1 large
　　pomegranate)

To reduce bitterness in walnuts, blanch them in boiling water for 3 minutes; drain thoroughly. To recrisp, spread nuts in a single layer on ungreased rimmed baking sheet; bake in a 350° oven for 8 minutes; set aside and reserve.

Melt butter in a wide frying pan over medium heat; add onion and cook, stirring, until onion is limp. Stir in flour, nutmeg, and pepper; cook until bubbly. Gradually stir in broth and cream until well blended. Cook, stirring constantly, until sauce bubbles and thickens; set aside to cool slightly, then refrigerate to chill completely. Stir in sour cream and salt to taste; cover and refrigerate as long as 1 day.

Slit chiles lengthwise, remove seeds, and pat chiles dry on paper towels. Arrange 10 of the chiles on a serving platter (about 13 to 15 inches in diameter) in spokelike fashion with tips hanging over edge of platter. Chop remaining chiles; toss them with turkey. Mound turkey mixture in center of platter; roll up tips of chiles to form a decorative rim. (Cover and chill if made ahead.)

Before serving, stir walnuts into chilled sour cream sauce; pour over mounded turkey, keeping chile rim exposed. Top evenly with pomegranate seeds.

To serve, use a pie server, making sure each guest gets a whole chile, some of the turkey and sauce, and pomegranate seeds. Makes about 10 servings.

Green Chile Stew

Chile Verde (*chee*-leh *ver*-deh)

Verde means "green" in Spanish. The verde in this meaty stew is supplied by fresh bell pepper, canned California green chiles, and chopped parsley. Make this dish ahead and reheat it at mealtime if you like. Serve it alone or over rice.

3 tablespoons olive oil or salad oil
1½ pounds *each* boneless beef chuck and
　　boneless, lean pork shoulder, cut in 1-inch
　　cubes
1 medium-size green bell pepper, seeded and
　　coarsely chopped
1 large clove garlic, minced or pressed
2 large cans (1 lb. 12 oz. *each*) tomatoes
1 large can (7 oz.) California green chiles,
　　seeded and chopped
⅓ cup chopped parsley
½ teaspoon sugar
¼ teaspoon ground cloves
2 teaspoons ground cumin or 1 tablespoon
　　whole cumin seed, crushed
1 cup dry red wine *or* ¼ cup lemon juice and ¾
　　cup regular-strength beef broth
　　Salt

Place a wide frying pan over medium-high heat, add oil, and brown half the meat at a time on all sides; remove with a slotted spoon and reserve. In pan drippings cook bell pepper and garlic until soft. In a large kettle (at least 5-qt. size) combine tomatoes (break up with a spoon) and their liquid, chiles, parsley, sugar, cloves, cumin, and wine. Bring tomato mixture to a boil, then reduce heat to a simmer. Add browned meats, their juices, cooked pepper and garlic. Cover and cook over low heat for 2 hours, stirring occasionally.

Remove cover; simmer for about 45 minutes more until sauce is reduced to thickness you wish and meat is fork tender. Add salt to taste. Makes 6 to 8 servings.

Chiles Rellenos

(*chee*-lehs rrreh-*yeh*-nohs)
Stuffed Peppers

Chiles rellenos or "stuffed peppers" are one of the best-known dishes served by Mexican restaurants in America. Usually they are stuffed with cheese to make chiles rellenos con queso. With this recipe you can make the cheese version or another kind, chiles rellenos con picadillo (peppers stuffed with a spicy ground beef mixture called picadillo).

To make chiles rellenos, you stuff the peppers, cover them with an egg batter, and fry. Here you have a

choice of three batters for three different kinds of coatings—thin and crispy, puffy, or omelet-like.

> 1 can (7 oz.) California green chiles or 6 to 8 fresh California green chiles, peeled (page 11)
> Cheese filling or picadillo filling (recipes follow)
> About ½ cup all-purpose flour, unsifted
> Thin and crispy coating, puffy coating, or omelet-like coating (recipes follow)
> Salad oil
> Salsa de jitomate (recipe follows), optional
> Garnishes: shredded jack cheese, sliced green onion tops, or Mexican red chile sauce (page 62 or canned)

Drain canned chiles and cut a slit down side of each; gently remove seeds and pith. Prepare fresh chiles, if used.

Stuff chiles with the filling of your choice. Slightly lap cut edges to hold filling inside. Roll each chile in flour to coat all over; gently shake off excess.

Prepare one of the suggested coatings just before you want to fry chiles. Coat and fry chiles according to instructions with each coating recipe.

If you like, top with hot salsa de jitomate and garnish with cheese and onion; or use Mexican red chile sauce. (Some prefer chiles rellenos without sauce, particularly the thin, crispy coated chile.) Serve immediately. Makes 3 or 4 servings.

Cheese filling. Stuff each chile with a piece of **jack cheese** about 1/2 inch wide, 1/2 inch thick, and 1 inch shorter than the chile. (Use a total of about 1/2 lb. jack cheese.)

Picadillo (pee-kah-*thee*-yoh) filling. Lightly toast 1/4 cup slivered **almonds** in 1 tablespoon **butter** or margarine in a frying pan over medium heat; remove almonds. Brown 1/2 pound lean **ground beef** in remaining butter. Add 1 minced or pressed clove **garlic**, 1/4 cup **tomato purée**, 1/4 cup seedless **raisins**, 2 tablespoons **dry sherry**, 1 teaspoon ground **cinnamon**, 1/2 teaspoon **salt**, 1/4 teaspoon ground **cloves**, 1 tablespoon **vinegar**, 1½ teaspoons **sugar**, and the almonds. Cook, uncovered, over medium heat for 20 minutes or until most liquid has evaporated. Cool. Fill each chile with about 2 teaspoons of filling.

Thin and crispy coating. Separate 5 **eggs**. Beat egg whites with 1 teaspoon **salt** until they hold firm, soft peaks. Using same beater, or a whip, beat egg yolks until thick; fold yolks into whites and use immediately.

Heat about 1/4 inch **salad oil** in a wide frying pan over medium heat. Coat chile all over with egg batter and use two forks to remove from batter. (If fresh chiles are used, hold each by its stem and just dip into batter—canned chiles have no such handy stems.)

Fry in hot oil just as many at one time as can be done without crowding. When each is golden brown on one side, turn over with a spatula and fork (or two spatulas) and fry until golden on the other side. Remove and drain briefly on paper towels.

Puffy coating. Separate 3 **eggs**. Beat whites until they form soft peaks. Beat yolks with 1 tablespoon **water**, 3 tablespoons all-purpose **flour**, and 1/4 teaspoon **salt** until thick and creamy; fold into whites.

Heat about 1½ inches of **salad oil** in a wide frying pan over medium heat. Dip stuffed chiles into the fluffy batter, place on a saucer, and slide into hot oil. When bottoms are golden brown, gently turn using a spatula and fork, and cook other side (3 to 4 minutes per side). Drain on paper towels.

Omelet-like coating. Separate 4 **eggs**. Beat whites until they form soft peaks. Beat egg yolks with 4 tablespoons all-purpose **flour**, 1 tablespoon **water**, and 1/4 teaspoon **salt**. Fold into whites.

Over medium heat, melt enough **butter** to coat bottom of omelet pan or frying pan. Make an oval mound of about 1/2 cup of the mixture. (You can cook each in a small omelet pan or 2 or 3 at a time in a wide frying pan.) Quickly lay a stuffed chile in center of mound and spoon about 1/3 cup mixture over top to encase chile. Cook for 2 to 3 minutes; gently turn and cook for 2 to 3 minutes longer or until golden.

Salsa de jitomate (*sahl*-sah deh hee-toh-*mah*-teh). In a frying pan over medium heat, cook 3 tablespoons finely chopped **onion** and 1 minced or pressed clove of **garlic** in 1 tablespoon **butter** or margarine until golden. Stir in 1 can (15 oz.) Spanish-style **tomato sauce**, 1/3 cup **water**, 1/4 teaspoon **salt**, and 1/4 teaspoon **oregano** leaves, crumbled. Simmer, uncovered, for 15 minutes. Serve hot. Makes 2½ cups.

Huevos rancheros offer many possible serving styles: a soft toasted corn tortilla, soft scrambled eggs, medium-hot sauce, and a garnish of avocado (recipe below). Accompany with shiny Oaxacan baked beans (page 68), flour tortillas (page 74), and hot chocolate (page 93).

Mexican Omelet

Tortilla de Huevos (tor-*tee*-yah deh *weh*-vohs)

The word "tortilla" not only applies to flat, round bread, it also can refer to an omelet (sometimes called a "tortilla de huevo" to distinguish it from the bread). Serve this omelet with refried beans and the familiar corn or flour tortillas.

    2 eggs, slightly beaten
    1 tablespoon *each* chopped green olives and
        seeded, chopped, canned California green
        chiles
    ¼ teaspoon salt
    2 teaspoons butter or margarine

To eggs add chopped olives, chiles, and salt. Melt butter in a small frying pan or 6 or 7-inch omelet pan over medium-high heat. When butter just begins to brown, pour in egg mixture all at once. As soon as bottom begins to set, lift edges to let uncooked portion flow into contact with center of pan. When eggs are set to your liking turn omelet out of pan. Makes 1 serving.

Huevos Rancheros

Ranch-style Eggs (*weh*-vohs rran-*che*-rohs)

Ranch-style (or farm-style eggs) can be served for any meal of the day in a variety of different ways. The cook has several options for preparing each element, such as the choice of tortillas, eggs, and sauces given here.

Tortillas and sauces can be made ahead; the eggs require last-minute cooking. Typical side dishes to serve with them are refried or black beans, or rice, or both. (See photograph at left.)

    Corn or flour tortillas (page 74 or purchased),
        reheated or fried (page 76)
    Eggs: fried, scrambled, or poached
        (directions follow)
    Sauces: mild, medium, or hot (directions
        follow)
    Garnishes: avocado slices or guacamole
        (page 9 or purchased), fresh coriander
        (cilantro), sliced radishes, shredded lettuce,
        chopped green onion, shredded jack or mild
        Cheddar cheese, lime wedges
    Tomato relish

For each serving place 1 or 2 cooked tortillas on a plate; top with 1 or 2 cooked eggs and about 1/2 cup of mild, medium, or hot sauce. Garnish with any suggested choices, and accompany with tomato relish.

Tortillas. As heated, stack tortillas in a covered dish or wrap in foil and keep hot up to 2 hours on electric warming tray or in warm oven.

Eggs. Cook until as set as you like.

Fried eggs. Melt 1 to 2 tablespoons **butter** or margarine in a wide frying pan over medium-low heat. (Use two pans to cook more than 6 eggs at one time.) Break in desired number of **eggs** and cook, uncovered, for sunnyside-up style until desired firmness. For opaquely covered yolks, sprinkle 1 to 2 tablespoons **water** into pan and cook, covered, until set as you like.

If desired, sprinkle each egg just as it begins to set with 1 tablespoon shredded **jack** or freshly grated Parmesan cheese.

Scrambled eggs. Melt 1 to 2 tablespoons butter or margarine in a wide frying pan over medium-low heat. With a fork blend 6 **eggs** with 2 tablespoons **water** and 1/2 teaspoon **salt**, or 12 eggs with 4 tablespoons water and 3/4 teaspoon salt. Pour eggs into pan with butter and cook until mixture turns opaque and begins to set on the bottom. Then push cooked portions aside with wide spatula, allowing uncooked egg to flow onto pan bottom. Repeat until eggs are cooked.

If desired, sprinkle eggs with 1/3 to 2/3 cup shredded **jack** or freshly grated Parmesan cheese just as they are almost firm; remove from heat, cover, and let stand about 1 minute to melt cheese.

Poached eggs. In a wide frying pan heat mild, medium, or hot sauce (recipes follow, use quantity given) until simmering. With back of a spoon make 6 evenly spaced depressions in sauce; break 1 **egg** into each depression. If desired, sprinkle each egg with 1 tablespoon shredded **jack** or freshly grated Parmesan cheese. Cover pan and cook on low heat until eggs are set.

Sauces. Chill, covered, if made ahead. Reheat if to be served hot.

Mild sauce. Mince 2 large **onions** and 1 seeded **green bell pepper**. In a wide frying pan, heat 3 tablespoons salad oil, add onion and pepper; cook, stirring, until soft. Add 1 can (14 oz.) pear-shaped **tomatoes** and their liquid, breaking tomatoes into small pieces with a spoon, and 1 can (about 14 oz.) regular-strength **chicken broth** or beef broth. Boil, uncovered, stirring to prevent sticking, until sauce is reduced to about $2^2/_3$ cups. Makes 6 servings.

Medium sauce. Prepare **mild sauce**, adding 1 to 2 cans (10 oz. *each*) **red chile sauce**, 1/2 teaspoon *each* **oregano** leaves, crumbled, and **cumin** seed; boil, uncovered, until reduced to about 3 cups; stir to prevent sticking. Makes 6 servings.

Hot sauce. Prepare medium sauce, adding 2 to 6 tablespoons chopped canned **California green chiles** (or add to taste). Boil, uncovered, until reduced to about 3 cups; stir to prevent sticking. Add addi-

 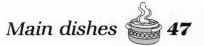

tional liquid **hot pepper seasoning** to taste. Makes 6 servings.

Tomato relish. Mince 1 large **tomato** and 6 to 8 **green onions** (include some tops) and mix with 2 to 4 tablespoons (or to taste) chopped canned **California green chiles**. Season with **salt** and **pepper** to taste. Serve cold. Makes about 1 cup.

Mayan Egg Tortillas

Tortillas de Huevo Maya
(tor-*tee*-yas deh *weh*-voh)

Unsalted pumpkin seeds (available in health food stores and some supermarkets) make a distinctive sauce for egg-stuffed flour tortillas. Served with a fresh fruit salad, this makes a good choice for brunch.

    8 ounces shelled, unsalted (untreated) pumpkin
        seeds (about 1½ cups)
    ½ cup regular-strength chicken broth
    3 tablespoons lemon juice
    1 clove garlic
    3 tablespoons seeded and chopped canned
        California green chiles
    ½ teaspoon salt
    1 teaspoon pepper
    1 cup whipping cream
    8 flour tortillas (page 74 or purchased)
    10 eggs
    2 tablespoons water
    2 tablespoons butter or margarine
    ⅓ cup chopped green onion

Whirl about half the pumpkin seeds in a blender container until coarsely chopped. Add chicken broth, lemon juice, garlic, chiles, salt, and pepper. Whirl until ingredients are well mixed. Add cream and whirl briefly, just to blend. Coarsely chop with a knife remaining pumpkin seeds and stir into cream mixture; set aside.

Follow directions for reheating tortillas (page 76).

Beat eggs and water together until well combined. Melt butter in wide frying pan over medium-low heat; pour in eggs and cook slowly, lifting cooked portion from pan with a wide spatula so uncooked eggs can flow underneath. Cook just until eggs are barely set and still moist on top. Remove pan from heat.

Spoon 1/8 of scrambled eggs down center of each tortilla; top each with about 2 tablespoons of sauce, roll to enclose filling, and arrange with seam side down in a 9 by 13-inch baking dish. Spoon remaining sauce over top.

Place in a preheated broiler 4 to 6 inches below heat and cook until sauce is lightly browned and mixture is heated through (4 to 6 minutes). Sprinkle with green onion and serve immediately. Makes 4 servings of 2 tortillas each.

Eggs with Avocado Sauce

Huevos con Salsa de Aguacates
(*weh*-vohs kohn *sahl*-sah deh ah-gooa-*kah*-tehs)

Hot hard-cooked eggs are clothed in green avocado sauce. A good choice for a special-occasion breakfast, these eggs could be accompanied by slices of fried ham or chorizo.

    2 tablespoons minced onion
    2 tablespoons butter or margarine
    1 canned California green chile, seeded and
        minced
    1 tablespoon all-purpose flour
    ½ cup milk
    8 hot hard-cooked eggs
    2 avocados, peeled, pitted, and cut in chunks
        Salt

In a small pan, cook onion in butter over medium heat until limp; add chile, flour, and milk. Cook, stirring, until thick (this much can be done ahead). Peel eggs; keep them warm in hot water while you complete sauce.

Whirl avocados smooth in a blender; stir into hot sauce. Season with salt to taste, and pour at once over hot, drained eggs. Makes 4 servings.

Montezuma Pie

Pastel deh Montezuma
(pas-*tehl* deh mohn-teh-*soo*-mah)

In Mexico, a pastel refers to any type of pie or casserole containing pastry or tortillas. This casserole, called pastel de Montezuma, layers corn tortillas with chunks of cooked turkey or chicken, sour cream, jack cheese, and a Mexican-flavored green sauce. You can make the green sauce quickly in your blender; start with a can of tomatillos (available in stores well stocked with Mexican products).

6 cups boned and skinned cooked turkey or chicken, cut into ½ by 2-inch pieces
Green sauce (directions follow)
1 pint (2 cups) sour cream
1 dozen corn tortillas (page 74 or purchased), cut into 1½-inch pieces
1½ pounds jack cheese, shredded or finely chopped

Arrange half the turkey pieces in a lightly greased 9 by 13-inch baking dish or a shallow 3-quart casserole. Spread over half the green sauce and half the sour cream; top with half the tortilla pieces and half the cheese. Repeat layers, using remaining turkey, green sauce, sour cream, and tortillas, ending with remaining cheese. Cover dish with foil; refrigerate until the next day, if desired. Bake, covered, in a 375° oven for 40 minutes (45 minutes if refrigerated); uncover and bake an additional 8 minutes or until cheese is bubbly and casserole is hot throughout. Cut into squares to serve. Makes 8 to 12 servings.

Green sauce. In a blender container, combine 1 can (14 oz.) Mexican **tomatillos,** drained; 1 small **onion,** cut in pieces; 2 cloves **garlic;** 1 can (4 oz.) whole **California green chiles,** pith and seeds removed; 1 bunch (about 1/2 cup) chopped fresh **coriander** (cilantro); 1 teaspoon **salt;** and 1/2 teaspoon **sugar.** Whirl until smooth.

Chiles Rellenos with Marinara Sauce

Chiles Rellenos con Salsa Marinara
(*chee*-lehs rreh-*yeh*-nohs kohn *sahl*-sa ma-ree-*na*-ra)

You can prepare this casserole in the morning or the night before. Bake just before serving. The soufflé-like casserole has layers of cheese-stuffed chiles under the egg and stays puffy about 5 minutes—long enough to bring to the table to serve. (See photograph on page 43.)

4 ounces jack cheese, cut in strips
1 can (4 oz.) California green chiles, seeds and pith removed
4 eggs
⅓ cup milk
½ cup all-purpose flour, unsifted
½ teaspoon baking powder
1 cup (about 4 oz.) shredded sharp Cheddar cheese
1 can (15 oz.) marinara sauce
Pitted ripe olives

Divide jack cheese evenly among chiles, folding or tucking cheese inside. Arrange chiles side by side in bottom of a greased, shallow 1½-quart baking dish.

With an electric mixer beat eggs until thick and foamy, then add milk, flour, and baking powder; beat until smooth as possible.

Pour egg batter over chiles, moistening evenly the surface of all chiles. Sprinkle with Cheddar cheese. Bake uncovered in a 375° oven for about 30 minutes or until casserole is puffed and appears set when gently shaken.

Just before casserole is ready, heat marinara sauce to simmering. Serve in a small container.

Garnish hot casserole quickly with olives and serve at once. Spoon portions of casserole over individual plates and pass marinara sauce to spoon onto servings as a topping. Makes 4 servings.

Chile con Carne

(*chee*-leh kohn *kar*-neh)

An American invention, chile con carne doesn't usually appear in Mexican cook books. Now well accepted south of the border, bowls of hot chile con carne are served by Mexican cooks, who top it with avocado slices and lots of fresh coriander leaves.

¾ teaspoon salt
1 pound lean ground beef
1 medium-size onion, chopped
1 can (14 oz.) pear-shaped tomatoes
1 large can (1 lb. 11 oz.) red kidney beans
1½ teaspoons chili powder
1 teaspoon oregano leaves, crumbled
½ teaspoon ground cumin seed
Avocado slices
¼ cup coarsely chopped fresh coriander (cilantro)

Heat salt in a wide frying pan over medium-high heat; crumble in ground beef and cook, stirring, until browned (about 5 minutes). Add onion and cook until limp. Discard any fat. Stir in tomatoes and their liquid, kidney beans and their liquid, chili powder, oregano, and cumin. Simmer, uncovered, stirring occasionally to break up tomatoes, for about 15 minutes. Garnish each serving with several avocado slices and pass coriander. Makes about 4 servings.

 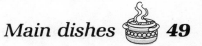

Tamales and Enchiladas

Slim or plump; rolled, folded, or stacked

Dried corn husks wrap around a coating of masa dough, sealing in a tasty filling and holding the concoction together while it is steam-cooked—that's a tamale.

For wrappers, any number of things can be used instead of corn husks—banana leaves, or even aluminum foil. And the choice of filling is up to you. But the masa dough can only be made from masa harina (also called dehydrated masa flour), a coarse flour made of specially prepared corn. There is no substitute which will give proper results. Steps for making tamales are covered at length in this chapter.

Other Mexican foods may rival the enchilada in popularity, but few, if any, can equal it in sheer number of variations. Enchiladas can be rolled, folded, or stacked with fillings of cheese, beans, meat, or all three, then garnished with a topping or sauce.

Mexican cooks have always been inventive, but for some reason enchiladas have inspired them to the highest flights of fancy.

Sauces and fillings for both tamales and enchiladas are in this chapter and can be used in other Mexican dishes.

Tamales

(tah-*mah*-les)

The tamale-making procedure is briefly this: Spread a corn husk with masa dough, put several spoonfuls of filling in center, then fold husk around filling to make a little packet. Stack packets in a steamer and steam until masa dough is cooked and firm.

Following are general directions for preparing husks, folding tamales, then steaming them.

(Note: *The Mexican singular is "tamal," but tamale has become the form used in the United States.)*

Corn husks for tamales. You can purchase dried husks in plastic bags or in bulk at many grocery and specialty food stores which handle Mexican foods. You can dry your own husks by leaving green husks in a warm, sunny spot for 3 to 8 days or until yellow; store in a dry place. (One pound of dried husks will make about 100 tamales.)

Fresh corn shucks can also be used. Many supermarkets strip them off before displaying corn and could save some at your request. However, American ears of corn, which are smaller than Mexican varieties, produce smaller husks. You will need to "patch" several together with masa dough as you make each tamale.

If corn husks are not available, you can use 6 by 8-inch pieces of foil, clear plastic film, or parchment paper. However, these materials do not contribute the authentic corn flavor, and the fact that they are nonporous causes the tamales to taste dry.

To prepare dry husks, soak in warm water just until pliable; remove any silks or extraneous materials and wash husks thoroughly. Don't worry about husks that have split, as two small pieces can be overlapped and used as one. Cover the husks with warm water and soak 2 hours to overnight. Keep damp until used.

Filling and folding tamales. For each tamale select a wide, pliable, soaked corn husk. Lay husk flat on the working surface with tip away from you.

Spread 2 tablespoons masa dough (page 52) on husk, in a rectangle about 5 by 4 inches. The greater dimension should be across the width of the husk. This rectangle of masa should be placed so that its right edge lies along the right edge of the husk, with margins of 2 or 3 inches at the bottom, at least 1 inch at the left side, and at least 2 inches at the top (generally much more).

If husk is not wide enough to provide for a rectangle of dough this size with ample margins, use some masa dough to paste another piece of husk onto the back of the first husk.

Spoon 2 tablespoons meat filling into the center of the masa rectangle. To enclose, fold right side over to center of filling; then fold left side over filling, allowing the plain part of the husk to wrap around tamale. Fold up bottom end over mound of dough-enclosed filling, then fold down the tip of the husk, wrapping it around the tamale if it is long enough. Lay tamale fold-side down to hold it shut. If necessary, you can tie it with a strip of thick husk about 1/4 inch wide.

Tamales may be made in other shapes, but this simple one is most typically Mexican.

(Continued on next page)

Spread masa dough *in a rectangle to right edge of a pliable, presoaked corn husk.*

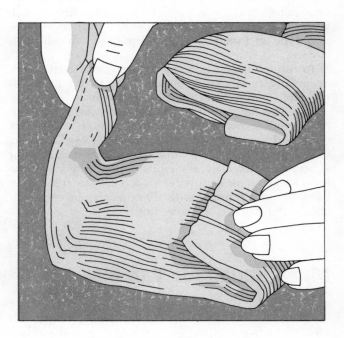

Fold bottom edge *over center, then fold down tip of husk. Lay tamale on tip to hold shut.*

Tamalitos. All tamales may be made in small size. Serve meat tamalitos as appetizers (you may want to add a few chopped canned California green chiles to the filling).

Shape tamalitos according to the preceding instructions for regular-size tamales. However, the corn husks should be about 2/3 the regular size (trim large ones with scissors if necessary) and for each tamalito, use only 1 tablespoon of masa dough spread in a 3½ by 2½-inch rectangle, and use 1 tablespoon meat filling. Tamalitos require almost as much cooking time as regular tamales.

Steaming tamales. Once tamales are folded, they are ready to steam. You can use a kettle designed for steaming or improvise one several ways. All you need is a rack placed above boiling water (at least 1 inch) and a lid or cover for container.

Use any large kettle or roasting pan. For the rack you can use any metal roasting rack, pressure cooker rack, or cake rack. Rest rack on tin cans of equal height with both ends removed. Be sure rack is well above water so it will not splash up onto tamales while boiling.

To steam, stack tamales on rack, folded side down; arrange them loosely enough so that steam can circulate freely. Cover kettle and place over medium heat so that water will boil gently.

The cooking time will vary according to the number of tamales you have stacked in the steamer, but will usually be about 45 minutes to 1 hour (add more boiling water as needed). To test for doneness, remove one tamale from the top and one from the center of the stack. Open them; they are done if masa dough is firm, does not stick to the shuck, and does not have a raw, doughy taste.

Tamales may be cooked ahead, then frozen. To do this, let tamales cool completely, then arrange a stack of about 6 on a rectangle of clear plastic film or foil. Wrap securely and seal with freezer tape. Record date and type of tamale. For best quality, use within 6 weeks.

To reheat frozen tamales, steam them, unthawed, according to the preceding directions for 20 to 30 minutes or until hot throughout.

After you have steamed the tamales, you might like to serve them with a sauce, even though this is not usually done in Mexico. You may heat Mexican red chile sauce (page 62 or canned) or canned enchilada sauce. Another easy, delicious sauce may be made from Mexican mole powder, which comes in 3-ounce cans. Simmer powder with 1½ cups regular-strength chicken or beef broth; serve hot.

Masa Dough for Tamales

If you need to double or triple the quantity of dough yielded by this recipe, still make batches with only 4 cups of masa flour at a time. The dough is very difficult to mix in a larger quantity.

1⅓ cups (⅔ lb.) lard, butter, margarine, or solid shortening
4 cups masa harina (dehydrated masa flour)
2 teaspoons salt
2⅔ cups warm water or regular-strength beef or chicken broth

Whip lard until fluffy. Blend in masa flour, salt, and warm water until dough holds together well.

Cover with damp cloth and keep cool until ready to use. Makes 6 cups or enough for 40 tamales (each using 2 tablespoons of prepared masa).

Fillings for Tamales

Ground beef filling and pork or chicken filling (page 64) are some basic filling recipes for tamales. Each recipe makes about 3 cups of filling, enough for about 20 tamales. The masa dough for meat tamales in the preceding recipe will make 40 tamales; therefore, you need to double either of the filling recipes to have enough to match that quantity of masa dough.

If you make as many as 200 tamales, an 18 to 20-pound turkey will supply enough meat and at the lowest cost. (You can even use the bones to make a stock which can be used for flavor in making the masa dough.)

Follow the basic procedure for making tamales (page 51) and use the fillings of your choice with prepared masa dough for meat tamales.

Colossal Chicken Tamales

Tamales de Pollo (tah-*mah*-les deh *poh*-yoh)

These big fat tamales are larger than the typical Mexican tamales. You will have to tie them shut with strips of corn husks. Serve them with rice and refried beans to complete the meal. (See photograph on page 70.)

Soaked dried corn husks (page 51)
Tamale masa dough (directions, page 53)
Chicken filling and chicken broth (directions, page 53)
1 tablespoon cornstarch blended with 1 tablespoon water
2 or 3 tablespoons canned green taco sauce
Sour cream (optional)

For each tamale, select 2 wide (or 3 smaller) soaked, dried corn husks and arrange them in a rectangle at least 10 inches wide. To do so, place husks side by side with the tip of each husk positioned by the base of the one next to it. Spread a little masa where husks overlap to seal; also use masa to mend tears. Place 1/3 cup masa in center of husk rectangle; spread masa in a 5 by

7-inch rectangle, making one edge of masa flush with one side of the husks.

Divide chicken filling in 12 equal portions and place one portion in center of each masa rectangle. Enclose filling according to directions for filling and folding tamales (page 51).

Tear another husk in thin strips and use strips to tie ends of tamale shut. Repeat to make each tamale.

Follow directions for steaming tamales (page 52) but increase cooking time to 1 hour and 20 minutes.

Meanwhile, blend cornstarch paste with 1¼ cups of the chicken broth reserved from chicken filling preparation (directions follow). Bring to a boil, stirring. Add 2 or 3 tablespoons green taco sauce.

Serve tamales hot; peel back husk and spoon some of the green taco sauce gravy onto each tamale and accompany with sour cream. Makes 12 tamales or 6 servings of 2 each.

Tamale masa dough. With an electric mixer, whip 1 cup (1/2 lb.) soft **butter** or margarine until fluffy; blend in 3 cups **masa harina** (dehydrated masa flour), 1 teaspoon **salt,** and 1¾ cups **chicken broth** reserved from chicken filling preparation (directions follow). Beat mixture until dough holds together well; use at once or cover and keep cool; return to room temperature to use. Makes about 4½ cups.

Chicken filling and chicken broth. Select 2 broiler-fryer **chickens** (about 3 lb. *each*), cut in pieces. Or buy 4 whole chicken legs with thighs attached and 2 large whole chicken breasts (about 4 lb. total).

Place all chicken pieces but breasts (reserve giblets for other uses) in a 5-quart kettle. Add 1 large, sliced **onion,** 3 whole cloves **garlic,** and 1 can (about 14 oz.) regular-strength **chicken broth.** Bring to a boil; cover and simmer, covered, for 25 minutes. Cut each breast

in half and add to kettle; continue to simmer, covered, for 20 minutes or until breasts have lost all pink color in thickest portions (cut a gash to test).

Lift chicken from broth and set aside to cool slightly, then pull off and discard skin and bones. Cut each breast section into 3 pieces; cut any other larger pieces of chicken into portions about the size of breast meat. (Cover and chill if made ahead.)

Pour chicken broth through wire strainer and reserve; discard vegetables. Measure broth; if you have less than 3 cups add water to make this total; if you have more than 3 cups, boil to reduce to this total. Cover and chill until ready to use.

Finely chop 1 large **onion** and cook until soft in 2 tablespoons **salad oil** in a wide frying pan over medium heat; add 1 large, seeded and slivered **green bell pepper** and 1 tablespoon **chili powder.** Cook, stirring, just until pepper is slightly limp but still bright green. Remove from heat and mix warm or cold chicken with cooked mixture and season with **salt** and **pepper** to taste.

Corn Tamales

Tamales de Maiz (tah-*mah*-lehs deh mah-*ees*)

Whole kernel and cream style corn are added to the usual masa flour in these tamales. Fingers of cheese and chile are the surprise ingredients inside.

> About 1 pound jack or Cheddar cheese
> 1 can (7 oz.) whole California green chiles, seeds and pith removed
> Soaked dried corn husks (page 51)
> Corn masa dough (directions follow)
> About 3 cups cooked chicken or turkey (torn into large, bite-size pieces)
> Canned green or red taco sauce
> Sour cream

Cut cheese into fingers about 1/2 inch thick and 2 inches long. Then cut or tear chiles into thin, lengthwise strips.

For each tamale, select 2 wide (or 3 smaller) soaked, dried corn husks. Arrange them side by side, placing the tip of each husk by the base of the one next to it to make a rectangle at least 10 inches wide. Where the husks overlap, spread a little of the corn masa dough (try to avoid the corn kernels, if possible) to join the two husks together; also use the masa dough to mend tears. Repeat process to make 16 corn husk rectangles.

In center of each husk rectangle place about 1/3 cup corn masa and spread into a 5 by 7-inch rectangle, making one edge of masa flush with one side of husks. Divide cheese, chiles, and chicken into 16 equal portions and place one portion of each in center of each masa rectangle. Enclose filling in masa coated section, matching masa at edges; then continue wrapping un-

coated portion of husk around outside of tamale.

Tear an extra tamale husk in thin strips and use strips to tie ends of tamale closed. Repeat to make each tamale.

Arrange tamales in a steamer, stacking them so steam can circulate. Or stack tamales in a 9 or 10-inch metal pie pan and place on rack in a large kettle over at least 1 inch of water. Cover steamer or kettle with a cloth, then set on lid. Steam over boiling water for about 1 hour and 30 minutes (add hot water as needed) or until corn husks peel readily from masa. To test, remove one tamale from top layer and let stand for about 5 minutes, then remove husk.)

Let tamales stand about 5 to 7 minutes before serving. Remove ties from ends and unwrap. Spoon taco sauce and sour cream onto each tamale. Makes 16 tamales or 8 servings of 2 each.

Corn masa dough. With an electric mixer, beat 3/4 cup **butter** or margarine until fluffy. By hand, beat in 1 can (1 lb. 1 oz.) *each* cream style **corn** and whole kernel **corn** (drained). In a separate bowl, stir together 1½ cups **masa harina** (dehydrated masa flour), 1/4 cup **sugar**, 2 teaspoons **salt**, and 1 tablespoon **baking powder**. Add to corn mixture alternately with 3/4 cup **milk**; beat well after each addition.

Quick Tamales

Tamales Rapidos (tah-*mah*-lehs *rah*-pee-thos)

The trick here is to use squares of foil as wrappers instead of the traditional corn husks. They steam just like regular tamales but are much quicker.

    2 cups masa harina (dehydrated masa flour)
    1¼ cups regular-strength chicken broth
    1½ teaspoons salt
    ½ cup salad oil
    2 cups cooked turkey or chicken, finely diced
    ½ cup pitted ripe olives, coarsely chopped
    1 medium-size onion, finely chopped
    ½ cup canned green chile salsa

Cut 30 pieces of foil, each 6 inches square. Stir together masa flour, chicken broth, 1/2 teaspoon of the salt, and oil to make a thick paste. Place about 1½ tablespoons of the paste on each foil square and spread in center of foil in a 3-inch square.

Mix together turkey, olives, onion, salsa, and the remaining teaspoon salt. Place about 1½ tablespoons of filling down center of each masa square. Fold foil edges together so masa edges meet, then seal all sides. Arrange tamales in steamer, stacking them so steam can circulate (see steaming tamales, page 52). Cover tightly and cook over 1 inch boiling water about 45 minutes or until masa is firm. Serve hot. Makes 2½ dozen small tamales (about 6 servings).

Enchiladas
(en-chee-*lah*-thas)

The ingredients for enchiladas are tortillas, a sauce, a filling, and sometimes a garnish or topping (or both).

To prepare them, dip tortillas in sauce and fry briefly in oil. To be neater but less traditional, fry tortillas and then dip in the sauce. Then roll, fold, or stack them with fillings such as cheese, beans, or meat.

In Mexico, enchiladas are served immediately after they are assembled. The American way, however, is geared to convenience. Just before serving pour more sauce over the dish and bake just long enough to heat all ingredients thoroughly. This means enchiladas can be assembled well ahead (as long as 24 hours) and reheated at the last minute.

Probably the greatest sins in enchilada-making are to fry the tortillas so long that they become crisp and to bake the dish so long that the tortillas dry out and get crusty on the edges.

Much debate has centered on the subject of how chile-pepper hot an enchilada should be. The traditional sauce contains a blend of bland red chile pulp and spices, which give rich seasoning without piercing sharpness. But if you are among those who like the pleasant torture of throat-searing hotness, add hot chiles or liquid hot pepper seasoning to the sauce, or select a very spicy filling, such as one made with chorizo.

Two enchiladas usually make an ample serving. Traditionally, the only accompaniments are refried beans and plain, hot tortillas, but most Mexican restaurants in America also serve rice and a salad.

Basic Enchilada Procedures

There are three basic steps to follow in making almost all kinds of enchiladas.

Frying tortillas. In a small frying pan, heat about 1/4 inch salad oil (Mexicans believe lard gives best results) over medium heat. Dip each tortilla into oil and fry a few seconds, until it begins to blister and becomes limp—*do not fry until firm or crisp.* Add more oil as needed. Remove with tongs and drain briefly.

Saucing tortillas. As soon as you take the tortilla out of the hot fat, dip it into the heated sauce each recipe specifies. A cake pan just larger than the tortilla is ideal for holding sauce. (Mexican cooks reverse the procedure and dip the tortilla in sauce before frying it in oil, but this causes so much splattering and mess that our recipes call for frying first.)

Filling and shaping enchiladas. Lay fried and sauced tortilla on a board or pan. Spoon required amount of filling, warm or cold, onto center. (Since the baking process will heat the filling through, it need not be hot, but it should not be icy cold.)

Enchiladas may be rolled, folded, or stacked. For rolled ones, turn part of tortilla over filling, roll, and place seam side down in a baking pan or on a heat-proof serving plate. Over the panful of enchiladas pour additional sauce—enough to make a shallow layer of sauce in the bottom of the pan and to moisten tortillas well so they will not dry out while baking.

For the folded kind, just fold each tortilla over filling to make half-moon shape and arrange neatly, slightly overlapping the one next to it. Pour additional sauce over the arranged enchiladas.

To make a "stack," spread filling and a little sauce evenly over each tortilla, and stack them in layers, spooning remaining sauce over stack. (When you serve, cut stack into wedges.)

Garnishing and baking enchiladas. Some garnishes—such as shredded cheese, chopped onions, and olives—are placed on top of the enchiladas before baking. After baking you can top with avocado slices, slivered radishes, sliced green onion, or slices of hard-cooked eggs or poached eggs.

Recipes vary, but a general rule for baking is to place enchiladas, uncovered, in a 350° oven about 20 minutes or just until thoroughly heated. Before baking, be sure tortillas are well moistened with sauce all over so that they will not dry or crisp on the edges.

Enchilada Variations

Tortillas. In addition to corn and flour tortillas, you may use a thin pancake or crepe of your own invention.

Sauces. You can purchase canned enchilada sauce or Mexican red chile sauce, or make a variety of sauces from recipes in this book.

Many Mexican cooks prefer a thinned mole sauce (page 37). Mole powder, made of a blend of spices, chiles, and ground chocolate (sometimes even ground nuts), is sold in little cans at Mexican and gourmet food shops. Prepare the sauce according to label instructions (or recipe, page 37) and thin with broth or water to the right consistency. (All enchilada sauces should be creamy and pourable.)

Other sauces can be based on the variety of canned tomato sauces now available, whipping cream or sour cream, canned green chile sauce, or other rich concoctions of your own invention.

Fillings. Choose from ground or slivered cooked meat and poultry, shredded cheese, onions, refried beans, green chiles, hard-cooked eggs, guacamole, or sour cream.

All fillings should be moist, but not runny. Sautéed onions or the sauce you use can be added to the filling for moisture. Raisins, nuts, olives, chopped vegetables, and many other tidbits can be added for flavor, color, and texture.

Topping and garnish variations. An unlimited variety of garnishes can be added for flavor or appearance after the dish is baked.

Around the enchiladas you could arrange borders of shredded or finely chopped raw vegetables and parsley. Mushrooms, currants, toasted nuts, capers, pickled chile peppers (red, green, or yellow, hot or mild), salami cut in thin strips, and crumbled bacon make excellent garnishes. Whatever your imagination suggests could be decorative.

You might even create a topping or sauce different from that used in the main recipe and serve it in a bowl alongside the enchiladas.

Rolled Beef Enchiladas

Enchiladas de Res Enrolladas
(en-chee-*lah*-thas deh rres en-roh-*yah*-thas)

Sour cream, cool and smooth, is spooned onto baked enchiladas for a pleasant flavor contrast. Red chile sauce you make yourself helps give this dish its special character, but you could substitute canned Mexican red chile or enchilada sauce if you wish.

16 corn tortillas (page 74 or purchased)
    Salad oil, shortening, or lard
    About 2½ cups Mexican red chile sauce (page 62 or canned), heated
3 cups ground beef filling (page 64)
¾ cup chopped onion
1½ cups (about 6 oz.) shredded sharp Cheddar cheese
2 cups sour cream

Fry tortillas in oil, and dip into heated chile sauce (see basic enchilada procedures, page 54).

Spoon about 3 tablespoons ground beef filling down center of each tortilla, and sprinkle with about 2 teaspoons onions. Roll tortilla around filling and place, seam side down, in an ungreased 9 by 13-inch baking dish. Place filled enchiladas side by side.

Pour enough sauce over enchiladas to moisten entire surface. Sprinkle with cheese. Bake, uncovered, in a 350° oven for 15 to 20 minutes or just until hot throughout. Serve with sour cream to spoon over individual servings. Makes 16 enchiladas (8 servings).

Stacked Cheese Enchiladas

Stacked Cheese Enchiladas

Enchiladas de Queso
(en-chee-*lah*-thas deh *keh*-soh)

Tortillas layered with filling are stacked one on top of the other and cut into pie-shaped wedges to serve. It is perhaps the easiest way to make enchiladas. (See photograph on page 67.)

- **12 corn tortillas (page 74 or purchased)**
  Salad oil, shortening, or lard
- **1½ cups Mexican red chile sauce (page 62 or canned), heated**
- **1½ cups (about 6 oz.) shredded sharp Cheddar cheese**
- **1 to 1½ cups chopped green onion, including some tops**

Fry tortillas in oil and dip into heated chile sauce (see basic enchilada procedures, page 54).

Place one tortilla in a small, shallow, ungreased baking dish; spoon over surface about 2 tablespoons shredded Cheddar, about 2 tablespoons chopped green onion, and a little of the chile sauce. Add remaining tortillas, preparing each layer the same way. Pour remaining sauce over stack, and top with remaining cheese.

Bake, uncovered, in a 350° oven for 15 to 20 minutes or until hot. Cut in wedges to serve. Serves 4.

Folded Pork Enchiladas

Enchiladas de Puerco Dobladas
(en-chee-*lah*-thas deh *puer*-koh doh-*blah*-thas)

To make these, you just fold the tortillas over the filling instead of rolling. Otherwise, the procedure is the same as for rolled beef enchiladas (page 55).

- **16 corn tortillas (page 74 or purchased)**
  Salad oil, shortening, or lard
- **2½ cups Mexican red chile sauce (page 62 or canned), heated**
- **3 cups pork filling (page 64)**
- **⅓ cup minced canned California green chiles, seeds and pith removed**
- **1½ cups (about 6 oz.) shredded jack cheese**

Fry tortillas in oil and dip into heated chile sauce (see basic enchilada procedures, page 54).

Spoon about 3 tablespoons pork filling and about 1 teaspoon minced chiles down center of each; fold tortilla over filling to make a half-moon shape. Arrange enchiladas, overlapping, in a shallow, ungreased 9 by 13-inch baking dish.

Pour over enough sauce to moisten entire surface. Sprinkle with cheese. Bake, uncovered, in a 350° oven for 15 to 20 minutes or just until heated through. Serve with bowl of heated sauce. Makes 16 enchiladas (8 servings).

Sour Cream Enchiladas

Enchiladas de Jocoque
(en-che-*lah*-thas deh hoh-*koh*-keh)

Sour cream both fills and garnishes these rich, less spicy, enchiladas, which are assembled a bit differently from most—pairs of overlapped tortillas are filled and folded. (See photograph on page 30.)

- **2 cups sour cream**
- **1 cup chopped green onion, including some tops**
- **½ teaspoon ground cumin**
- **4 cups (about 16 oz.) shredded Longhorn Cheddar cheese**
- **12 corn tortillas (page 74 or purchased)**
  Salad oil, shortening, or lard
- **1 can (10 oz.) enchilada sauce, heated**
  Sour cream and chopped green onion

Blend the 2 cups sour cream, 1 cup chopped onion, cumin, and 1 cup of the shredded cheese.

Fry tortillas in oil and dip in heated enchilada sauce (see basic enchilada procedures, page 54).

In an ungreased 7 by 11-inch baking dish, overlap two tortillas at one end of dish, allowing part of tortillas to extend over edge of dish. Spread about 6 tablespoons of sour cream filling down center of tortillas, and fold extending sections down over filling.

Repeat this technique to fill remaining tortillas, placing them side by side and completely covering dish bottom; use all filling. Sprinkle remaining 3 cups cheese evenly over top. (Cover and chill up to 3 or 4 hours, if made ahead.)

Bake, uncovered, in a 375° oven for 20 minutes (30 minutes, if chilled) or until hot throughout. Garnish with dollops of sour cream spooned down center of enchiladas. Sprinkle with green onions. Makes 6 enchiladas (about 6 servings).

Cheese Enchiladas

Enchiladas de Queso
(en-chee-*lah*-thas deh *keh*-so)

These enchiladas, with a substantial filling of cheeses and onions, make a sturdy luncheon or supper entrée. Offer a crisp green salad and fresh fruit or sherbet for dessert.

- **12 corn tortillas (page 74 or purchased)**
  Salad oil
- **1 can (7 oz.) green chile salsa**
  Cheese filling (directions follow)
- **2 cups (about 8 oz.) shredded Longhorn Cheddar cheese**
  Garnishes: about 1 cup finely shredded iceberg lettuce; 2 medium-size tomatoes, thinly sliced; about ¼ cup thinly sliced green onion, including some tops; 1 tablespoon vinegar; salt

Fry tortillas in oil (see basic enchilada procedures, page 54).

Pour about 1/3 of the green chile salsa in the bottom of a 9 by 13-inch baking dish. Barely overlap two tortillas in dish bottom. Spoon about 2/3 cup filling across overlapped tortillas, fold over, and slide to one end of dish. Repeat this technique to fill remaining tortillas; overlap each pair of tortillas and place them side by side to completely cover dish bottom.

Tuck ends under last set of enchiladas. Moisten surface of enchiladas with remaining green chile salsa and cover with shredded cheese. (Cover and chill as long as 24 hours, if made ahead.)

Bake, uncovered, in a 375° oven for 20 minutes or until bubbling (if chilled, bake 30 minutes, covered, for the first 15 minutes). Garnish enchiladas with lettuce, tomatoes, and green onion. Sprinkle vinegar and salt over vegetables. Makes 12 enchiladas (about 6 servings).

Cheese filling. Stir together to blend 1½ pints (3 cups) large curd **cottage cheese,** 1 cup (about 4 oz.) shredded **Longhorn Cheddar cheese,** 1½ cups finely chopped **green onion** (including some tops), and 1/4 teaspoon **oregano** leaves, crumbled.

Meat-Raisin Enchiladas

Enchiladas de Picadillo
(en-chee-*lah*-thas deh pee-kah-*dee*-yoh)

Raisins add a pleasing, sweet accent to the meat filling for these enchiladas.

- **Warm water**
- **¼ cup raisins**
- **2 cups finely diced cooked beef or pork**
- **¼ cup minced onion**
- **About 3 cups chile-tomato sauce (page 63), heated**
- **12 corn tortillas (page 74 or purchased)**
  Salad oil, shortening, or lard
- **12 pitted ripe olives**

Run warm water over raisins to plump them; drain. Mix raisins with meat, onion, and 1/3 cup of the sauce. Set aside. Pour about 1/2 cup sauce into a 9 by 13-inch baking dish; set aside.

Fry tortillas in oil and dip in remaining chile-tomato sauce (see basic enchilada procedures, page 54). Roll about 3 tablespoons filling and an olive into each tortilla and arrange, seam side down, in sauce-lined baking dish. Pour all remaining sauce evenly over top.

Bake, uncovered, in a 350° oven for 15 to 20 minutes or until heated through. Makes 12 enchiladas (4 to 6 servings).

Chicken Enchiladas, Uruápan

Enchiladas de Pollo de Uruapan
(en-chee-*lah*-thas deh *poh*-yoh deh co-roo-*ah*-pan)

Cheese is the filling for the tortillas; chicken legs, simmered in a chile sauce until tender, are served on top. If you wish, you can cook the chicken ahead and refrigerate it in the sauce.

- **6 whole chicken legs (including thighs)**
  Salt
  Salad oil
- **1 small onion, finely chopped**
- **1¼ cups Mexican red chile sauce (page 62 or canned), heated**
- **¼ cup water**
- **12 corn tortillas (page 74 or purchased)**
- **¾ cup grated Romano cheese**
- **2 cups (about 8 oz.) shredded jack cheese**
  Garnishes: whole radishes, cucumber slices, lime wedges

Sprinkle chicken pieces lightly with salt. Heat 2 tablespoons oil in a wide frying pan over medium-high heat and brown chicken well on all sides. Discard excess fat. Add onion, red chile sauce, and water, stirring to blend. Cover pan and simmer gently for about 30 minutes or until thigh meat is no longer pink near bone when slashed. (At this point you can chill chicken in sauce as long as 24 hours, then reheat to simmering and continue.) Remove chicken from sauce and keep warm; reserve sauce.

Fry tortillas in oil and dip into heated chile sauce (see basic enchilada procedures, page 54). Stack tortillas as you go (they tear easily).

Mix Romano and jack cheese; spoon 2 generous tablespoons of cheese down center of each tortilla and fold in half over filling. Arrange enchiladas, overlapping, on large heat-proof serving platter or large baking dish and place chicken alongside or on top. Spoon on remaining sauce and sprinkle with balance of cheese.

Bake, uncovered, in a 350° oven for 15 minutes or until heated through. Garnish with radishes, cucumbers, and lime wedges. Squeeze lime onto individual servings. Makes 12 enchiladas (6 servings).

Enchiladas de Res y Frijoles Refritos
(en-chee-*lah*-thas deh free-*hoh*-less rrreh-*free*-tohs)

You could serve these for a buffet meal, letting each person help himself to the sour cream and chile sauce toppings. If you wish, you can assemble this enchilada casserole and refrigerate it for several hours, or overnight, before baking.

1½ pounds lean ground beef
1 medium-size onion, chopped
2 cups refried beans (page 68 or canned)
1 teaspoon salt
⅛ teaspoon garlic powder
⅓ cup bottled or canned taco sauce
1 cup quartered, pitted ripe olives
12 corn tortillas (page 74 or purchased)
Salad oil, shortening, or lard
2 cans (10 oz. *each*) enchilada sauce
3 cups (about 12 oz.) shredded Cheddar cheese
Sliced, pitted ripe olives
Sour cream
Canned green chile salsa

In a wide frying pan, crumble in ground beef and add onion. Cook over medium-high heat until meat is browned and onion is limp. Stir in beans, salt, garlic powder, taco sauce, and quartered olives; heat until bubbly.

Fry tortillas in oil (see basic enchilada procedures, page 54).

Heat enchilada sauce; pour about half into an ungreased, shallow 9 by 13-inch baking dish.

Place about 1/3 cup of the ground beef filling on each tortilla and roll to enclose. Place, seam side

down, in sauce in bottom of baking dish. Pour remaining enchilada sauce evenly over tortillas; cover with cheese. (Cover and chill as long as 24 hours, if made ahead.) Bake, uncovered, in a 350° oven for about 15 to 20 minutes or until thoroughly heated. (If chilled, bake 45 minutes.)

Garnish with olive slices. Spoon sour cream and green chile salsa over each serving. Makes 12 enchiladas (about 4 to 6 servings).

Enchiladas de Chorizo
(en-chee-*lah*-thas deh cho-*ree*-soh

In some parts of Mexico and the southwestern United States, chorizo refers not only to the spicy link sausage but also to a highly seasoned ground meat mixture sold fresh just as regular bulk sausage. You make just such a chorizo mixture to fill these enchiladas.

The Longhorn Cheddar cheese specified has better melting qualities than other Cheddars and more closely resembles the cheese used in Mexico.

Bulk chorizo filling (page 64) or about 1½
pounds purchased chorizo, skinned
1½ cups (about 6 oz.) *each* shredded jack and
Longhorn Cheddar cheese
12 corn tortillas (page 74 or purchased)
Salad oil, shortening, or lard
1 can (10 oz.) enchilada sauce, heated
1 cup sour cream
Pitted ripe olives
1 cup guacamole (page 9 or purchased)

Prepare chorizo filling, breaking meat apart as it cooks. Cool filling slightly and stir in 1/2 cup *each* of the jack and Cheddar cheeses.

Fry tortillas in oil and dip into heated enchilada sauce (see basic enchilada procedures, page 54).

In a 9-inch-square, ungreased baking pan, overlap

two tortillas to extend across one side of pan, allowing part of tortillas to extend over rim. Spoon 1/6 of the meat mixture down center of tortillas and fold over filling. Repeat this technique to fill remaining tortillas, placing them side by side, completely covering pan bottom. Pour any remaining sauce over top. Sprinkle top with remaining cheese. (Cover and chill if made ahead.)

Bake, uncovered, in a 350° oven for 30 minutes or until heated through. (If chilled, bake 50 minutes, keeping covered first 20 minutes.) Spoon over dollops of sour cream, top with olives, and serve with guacamole. Makes 12 enchiladas (8 servings).

Chicken Cream Enchiladas

Enchiladas de Pollo y Crema
(en-chee-*lah*-thas deh *poh*-yoh ee *kreh*-mah)

Lumps of warm, soft cream cheese are interlaced with bits of chicken, sweet, slow-cooked onions, and mellow red peppers. These hearty enchiladas are special enough for a company entrée.

    12 corn tortillas (page 74 or purchased)
        Salad oil
        Cream cheese chicken filling
            (directions follow)
    ⅔ cup whipping cream
     2 cups (about 8 oz.) shredded jack cheese
        Garnishes: radishes, pitted ripe olives, fresh
            coriander (cilantro)
        Lime wedges

Fry tortillas in oil (see basic enchilada procedures, page 54).

Spoon about 1/3 cup of the chicken filling down center of each tortilla and roll to enclose. Set enchiladas, seam side down, in a 9 by 13-inch baking dish, side by side. (Cover and chill, if made ahead.)

Moisten tops of enchiladas with whipping cream, then sprinkle cheese evenly over them. Bake, uncovered, in a 375° oven for 20 minutes to heat through. (If chilled, bake for 30 minutes; cover casserole for first 15 minutes.) Garnish with radishes, olives, and coriander before serving. Pass lime wedges to squeeze onto individual servings. Makes 12 enchiladas (about 6 servings.)

Cream cheese chicken filling. In a wide frying pan over medium heat, cook 2 large **onions**, thinly sliced, in 2 tablespoons **butter** or margarine, stirring occasionally, for about 20 minutes or until limp and just beginning to brown. Remove from heat and add 2 cups diced, **cooked chicken** (skin removed); 1/2 cup canned, roasted **sweet red pepper** or pimento, chopped; and 2 small packages (3 oz. *each*) **cream cheese**, diced. Mix lightly with two forks to blend, then season with **salt** to taste.

Acapulco Enchiladas

Enchiladas de Acapulco
(en-chee-*lah*-thas deh ah-kah-*pool*-koh)

Slivered almonds give a pleasing crunchiness to the rich filling in these enchiladas, named for their place of origin.

    2 cups diced cooked chicken or turkey
    ½ cup chopped ripe olives
    1 cup slivered or coarsely chopped almonds
    3 cups canned enchilada sauce or Mexican red
        chile sauce (page 62 or canned), heated
    12 corn tortillas (page 74 or purchased)
        Salad oil
    1½ cups (about 6 oz.) shredded sharp Cheddar
        cheese
    2 cups sour cream
    4 tablespoons minced green onion

Combine chicken, olives, almonds, and enough sauce to moisten (about 1/3 cup); set aside.

Fry tortillas in oil and dip into heated enchilada sauce (see basic enchilada procedures, page 54).

Evenly spoon chicken mixture down center of each tortilla and roll to enclose. Place enchiladas, seam side down, in a shallow ungreased 9 by 13-inch baking dish. Top with remaining sauce and sprinkle with cheese.

Bake, uncovered, in a 350° oven for 15 to 20 minutes or until heated through. Mix sour cream with onion and serve cold to spoon over. Makes 12 enchiladas (about 4 to 6 servings).

Souffléed Green Chile Enchilada

Enchiladas de Chile Verde
(en-chee-*lah*-thas deh *chee*-leh *ver*-deh)

Quite unlike a typical enchilada, this casserole consists of a puffy egg mixture—resembling a soufflé, but more stable—baked in a tortilla-lined dish. The casserole goes well with simply roasted or grilled meats or poultry, or it can be a main dish for a light meal.

    7 or 8 corn tortillas (page 74 or purchased)
        Salad oil
    1 can (7 oz.) green chile salsa, heated
    4 eggs, separated
    1 tablespoon all-purpose flour
    1¾ cups (about 8 oz.) shredded jack cheese
        3 to 4 canned California green chiles (seeds
            and pith removed), chopped
    1 mild pickled red chile pepper

Fry tortillas in oil and dip in heated green chile sauce (see basic enchilada procedures, page 54).

(Continued on next page)

Put 1 tortilla in bottom of a 7 or 8-inch ungreased baking dish (at least 2 inches deep); arrange remaining tortillas, overlapping, around sides and slightly over bottom center tortilla.

Beat egg whites until stiff; set aside. With same beater whip egg yolks until slightly thickened, then beat in flour; stir in 1 cup of the cheese, chopped chiles to taste, and little of the egg white. Fold yolk mixture into remaining whites and pour into tortilla-lined dish.

Fold tortillas down over filling. Spoon remaining salsa over tortillas, then sprinkle evenly with remaining cheese.

Bake, uncovered, in a 375° oven for 30 minutes. Garnish with red pepper and serve. Makes 4 main-dish or 6 side-dish servings.

Fresh Corn Enchiladas

Enchiladas de Maiz Fresco
(en-chee-*lah*-thas deh mah-*ees fres*-koh)

Offer these vegetable enchiladas to accompany barbecued or roasted meats, such as beef, chicken, or ham.

    12 corn tortillas (page 74 or purchased)
       Salad oil
     1 can (10 oz.) enchilada sauce or about 1 cup
       Mexican red chile sauce (page 62 or canned)
       Fresh corn filling (recipe follows)
     2 cups (about 8 oz.) shredded jack cheese
       About 1 cup finely shredded iceberg lettuce
     1 cup sour cream
    ⅓ cup minced fresh coriander (cilantro)
       Lime wedges

Fry tortillas in oil (see basic enchilada procedures, page 54).

Pour about 1/3 of the enchilada sauce in the bottom of a 9 by 13-inch baking dish.

Spoon about 1/3 cup of fresh corn filling down center of each tortilla, rolling to enclose. Set enchiladas seam-side down in sauce, arranging side by side in dish. Moisten tops of enchiladas evenly with remaining sauce. Distribute cheese evenly over enchiladas. (Cover and chill, if made ahead.) Bake, uncovered, in a 375° oven for 20 minutes or until bubbling (if chilled bake 30 minutes, covered for the first 15 minutes).

To serve, arrange a band of lettuce down center of enchiladas, then spoon sour cream onto lettuce. Garnish with coriander and squeeze lime juice onto individual portions. Makes 12 enchiladas (about 6 servings).

Fresh corn filling. Cut off enough **fresh corn kernels** to make 3 cups (about 6 medium-size ears). In a wide frying pan, melt 2 tablespoons **butter** or margarine and add 3 medium-size **onions,** finely chop-

ped. Cook, stirring, until onion is limp but not browned. Add corn, 1/2 teaspoon **cumin** seed, and 1/4 cup **water.** Cover and cook over medium heat for about 5 minutes, stirring occasionally. Remove cover and cook, stirring, over high heat to boil away any remaining liquid.

Remove from heat and stir in 1 cup **sour cream,** 1 cup (about 4 oz.) shredded **jack cheese,** and 1/4 to 1 can (4 oz.) **California green chiles,** chopped (seeds and pith removed). Taste as you add chiles to determine how hot you want it. Season with **salt** to taste.

Spinach Enchiladas

Enchiladas de Espinaca
(en-chee-*lah*-thas deh es-pee-*nah*-ka)

A departure from the more familiar enchilada combinations, these enchiladas combine three tasty partners—spinach, ground beef, and cheese.

    1½ teaspoons salt
      2 pounds lean ground beef
      1 large onion, chopped
      1 package (10 oz.) frozen chopped spinach,
        thawed
      1 teaspoon oregano leaves
     ¼ teaspoon pepper
     ½ cup grated Parmesan cheese
      2 cans (10¾ oz. *each*) condensed tomato soup
      1 can (10 oz.) enchilada sauce
     12 corn tortillas (page 74 or purchased)
      1 can (6 oz.) pitted ripe olives, drained
      2 cups (about 8 oz.) shredded jack cheese

Heat salt in a wide frying pan over medium heat; add beef and cook until crumbly. Discard all but 2 tablespoons drippings. Add onion, spinach, oregano, pepper, and Parmesan cheese; cover and cook until spinach is hot through.

Meanwhile, combine tomato soup and enchilada

sauce in a pan; simmer over low heat, uncovered, for 10 minutes. Dip each tortilla in sauce until limp, lay on a plate, and spoon about 1/2 cup of meat mixture down center of tortilla. Top with 3 or 4 olives, roll, and arrange seam side down in a shallow 3-quart baking dish. Pour remaining sauce evenly over top. Bake, uncovered, in a 350° oven 30 minutes or until sauce is bubbly.

Sprinkle jack cheese evenly over top; bake 5 minutes more or until cheese is melted. Makes 12 enchiladas (6 servings).

Chile and Cheese Enchiladas

Enchiladas de Chile y Queso
(en-chee-*lah*-thas deh *chee*-leh e *keh*-soh)

Roll soft tortillas around a creamy cheese filling robustly seasoned with chiles. Then sprinkle more cheese on top just before baking.

1½ cups *each* sour cream and small curd cottage cheese
1 envelope (1 oz.) instant onion soup (amount for 1 serving)
1 cup finely chopped green onion
12 corn tortillas (page 74 or purchased)
  Salad oil
1 large can (7 oz.) California green chiles, seeded and cut in 12 thick strips
1 pound jack cheese, shredded
1 can (10 oz.) enchilada sauce

In a bowl combine sour cream, cottage cheese, onion soup, and green onions; set aside.

Fry tortillas in oil (see basic enchilada procedures, page 54). Spoon about 1/4 cup of sour cream mixture down center of each tortilla; top with 1 green chile strip, then add about 1/4 cup of the jack cheese. Roll up and place side by side, seam side down, in a 9 by 13-inch baking pan. Spoon remaining sour cream mixture evenly over tortillas, then pour enchilada sauce over them and sprinkle remaining jack cheese over all.

Bake, uncovered, in a 350° oven for 30 minutes or until bubbly. Let stand 5 to 10 minutes before serving. Makes 12 enchiladas (6 servings).

All-American Enchiladas

Enchiladas de los Estados Unidos
(en-chee-*lah*-thas deh lohs es-*tah*-thos oo-*nee*-thos)

Canned chile con carne is spooned over frankfurters, and the combination is rolled in a tortilla, topped with

sauce, and baked. You can use regular or garlic frankfurters or smoked sausage links.

1 tablespoon salad oil
1 small onion, chopped
¼ cup seeded and chopped canned California green chiles
1 large can (15 oz.) tomato sauce
4 to 6 drops liquid hot pepper seasoning
12 corn tortillas (page 74 or purchased)
12 frankfurters
2 cans (15 oz. *each*) chile con carne
2 cups (about 8 oz.) shredded Cheddar or jack cheese

Pour oil into a wide frying pan over medium heat; add onion and sauté until limp. Stir in chiles, tomato sauce, and hot pepper seasoning; heat to simmering.

Dip each tortilla into sauce; drain briefly. Place frankfurter on top and spoon over about ¹/₁₂ of the chile con carne, then sprinkle with about 1½ tablespoons of the cheese. Roll tortillas and place, seam side down, in a greased 9 by 13-inch baking pan. Pour remaining sauce over all.

Cover and bake in a 350° oven for 25 minutes. Uncover, sprinkle with remaining cheese, and bake for 5 minutes more or until cheese is melted. Makes 12 enchiladas (6 servings).

Egg Enchiladas

Enchiladas de Huevos
(en-chee-*lah*-thas deh *weh*-vohs)

Softly scrambled eggs are rolled up inside these enchiladas. They don't bake. Just slip them under a broiler to melt the cheese.

2 tablespoons salad oil
1 medium-size onion, chopped
1 green pepper, seeded and chopped
3 cans (8 oz. *each*) tomato sauce
2 teaspoons chili powder
8 eggs
¼ cup half-and-half (light cream) or milk
2 tablespoons chopped canned California green chiles
  Salt and pepper
2 tablespoons butter or margarine
6 corn tortillas (page 74 or purchased)
1 cup (about 4 oz.) shredded Cheddar cheese

Heat oil in a wide frying pan over medium heat and sauté onion and green pepper until limp; add tomato sauce and chili powder. Simmer, uncovered, for about 10 minutes.

Beat eggs lightly with half-and-half; add chiles, and salt and pepper to taste. In another frying pan over medium-low heat, melt butter, add eggs and cook until set to your liking. Dip each tortilla in hot tomato sauce until soft, and spoon ⅙ of the scrambled eggs down center. Roll up and place seam side down in a shallow baking dish. Reheat remaining sauce to boiling, pour over top, and sprinkle with cheese. Place under broiler 4 inches from heat until cheese melts (about 3 minutes). Makes 6 enchiladas (3 to 6 servings).

Enchilada Pie

Pastel de Enchilada
(pah-*stel* deh en-chee-*lah*-tha)

Quick and easy, this casserole can be prepared and on the table in half an hour. Cut into wedges to serve.

    1 pound lean ground beef
    1 onion, chopped
    1 teaspoon salt
    ¼ teaspoon pepper
    1 tablespoon chili powder
    1 can (8 oz.) tomato sauce
    6 corn tortillas (page 74 or purchased)
      Butter or margarine
    1 can (4½ oz.) chopped black olives
 1½ cups (about 6 oz.) shredded sharp Cheddar
      cheese
    ½ cup water

In a wide frying pan over medium-high heat, brown beef and onion. Add salt, pepper, chili powder, and tomato sauce.

Spread each tortilla with butter. In a 2-quart casserole, alternate layers of buttered tortillas, meat sauce, olives, and cheese. Add water, cover, and bake in a 400° oven for 20 minutes. Makes 4 to 6 servings.

Sauces and Fillings

Some of these sauces, particularly the thick, moist ones of meat or beans, are used more as fillings—in tacos, tamales, or enchiladas. All these sauces and fillings have a variety of uses, and are called for in a number of recipes throughout this book.

Tomato & Green Chile Sauce

Salsa Cruda (*sahl*-sah *kroo*-thah)

A bowl of sauce often is a standard feature on a Mexican table. Serve this colorful fresh sauce for diners to spoon onto their food to suit their own taste. You can make it as hot as you like, depending on the number of chiles you use.

    6 medium-size tomatoes, peeled and finely
      chopped
    ½ cup (or more) thinly sliced or diced canned
      California green chiles (seeds and pith
      removed) or fresh chiles (directions for
      peeling, page 11)
    ⅓ cup minced onion
    1 teaspoon salt
      Minced canned jalapeño chiles (or other hot
      chiles)

Mix tomatoes with green chiles, onion, salt, and jalapeño chiles to taste (about 1 jalapeño to each cup of sauce will make it noticeably hot). Makes about 3 cups.

Mexican Red Chile Sauce

Salsa de Chile Rojo
(*sahl*-sah deh *chee*-leh *rro*-ho)

Dip tortillas in this cooked sauce to make enchiladas. Moisten meat fillings with it. Or serve it as a condiment with meats. You can buy a similar sauce in cans, but the sauce you make yourself is milder, thicker, and more flavorful—and you can freeze part to use later. Preparing the chiles is somewhat messy if you don't have a blender. Be sure to get the right dried chiles— large, dusky-red, mild ones, usually found only at stores specializing in Mexican foods.

6 ounces (about 10 to 12) whole dried ancho, pasilla, or California green chiles (or a mixture of all three)
3 cups hot water
¼ cup tomato sauce or tomato paste
1 small clove garlic, minced or pressed
¼ cup salad oil
1½ teaspoons salt
1 teaspoon oregano leaves, crumbled
¼ teaspoon ground cumin

Place chiles on a baking sheet. Toast lightly in a 400° oven for 3 or 4 minutes only or until they give off a mild aroma. If burned, chiles will be very bitter.

Remove from oven, let cool to touch, then remove and discard stems, seeds, and any pink pithy material inside chiles. Rinse in cool water, drain briefly, then cover chiles with hot water; let stand 1 hour.

Place chiles in a blender with enough of the water to blend; whirl until smooth. (Or scrape pulp from skin with table knife, then put through a wire strainer.) Add remaining water, tomato sauce, garlic, oil, salt, oregano, and cumin. Simmer, uncovered, for 10 minutes, stirring occasionally, to blend flavors. Chill up to 1 week or freeze for longer storage. Makes 3½ cups.

Green Tomatillo Sauce

Salsa de Tomatillo
(*sahl*-sah deh toh-mah-*tee*-yoh)

This subtly flavored, thick sauce is quite simple to make if you can find the necessary canned tomatillos (small, tart green tomatoes).

Don't try to substitute ordinary green tomatoes—they do not have the proper taste or dense texture.

For an entrée, heat cooked pork, turkey, or chicken in the sauce or serve the sauce separately with roasts or grilled meats. It is also complementary to beef, lamb, and particularly venison.

1 medium-size onion, finely chopped
¼ cup finely chopped blanched almonds
2 tablespoons salad oil
2 cans (10 oz. *each*) tomatillos
1 tablespoon minced fresh coriander (cilantro) or 1 teaspoon ground coriander
About 3 tablespoons minced canned California green chiles, seeds and pith removed
2 cups regular-strength chicken broth

Combine onion, almonds, and oil in a pan over medium heat and cook, stirring, until onion is limp and almonds are lightly browned.

Whirl tomatillos and their liquid in blender until mixture is fairly smooth (or rub through wire strainer, using all liquid and pulp); add to onion mixture. Stir in coriander and chiles to taste. (The sauce should be fairly mild.)

Add chicken broth and boil rapidly, uncovered, until reduced to about 2½ cups; stir occasionally. Makes about 2½ cups.

Chile-Tomato Sauce

Salsa de Chile y Tomate
(*sahl*-sah deh *chee*-leh ee toh-mah-teh)

Chili powder instead of a paste from dried chiles makes this sauce easy to prepare. The recipe makes enough sauce for 20 enchiladas.

1 medium-size onion, minced
2 tablespoons salad oil
3½ cups tomato purée
2 cloves garlic, minced or pressed
4 tablespoons chili powder
½ teaspoon ground cumin
¼ teaspoon oregano leaves, crumbled
1 teaspoon salt

In a pan, cook onion in oil over medium heat just until limp. Add tomato purée and garlic. Gradually stir in chili powder. Add cumin, oregano, and salt. Cover and simmer for 30 minutes, stirring frequently, to blend flavors. Pour through wire strainer. Makes about 3 cups.

"Little Meats" Pork

Carnitas
(kar-*nee*-tas)

The name of this succulent dish means "little meats." The pork is so tender it is easily cut into chunks or shredded into little pieces good for a taco filling. It also can be served like a roast.

4½ to 5-pound bone-in pork shoulder
Water
2 teaspoons salt
½ teaspoon *each* ground cumin, ground coriander, and oregano leaves, crushed
2 medium-size onions, chopped
2 carrots, chopped

Place pork in a deep pan and just barely cover with water. Add salt, cumin, coriander, oregano, onion, and carrots. Bring water to a boil, cover pan, reduce heat, and simmer for 2½ hours or until fork tender. Lift meat from stock (save for soups) and place in a shallow baking pan.

Bake, uncovered, in a 350° oven for 45 minutes to 1 hour or until meat is very well browned. Drain off all fat. Shred or separate meat into chunks to serve. Makes 6 to 8 servings.

Ground Beef Filling

Relleno de Carne Picada
(rreh-*yeh*-noh deh *kar*-neh pee-*kah*-thah)

Browned ground beef, seasoned with onion and red chile sauce, makes a tasty all-purpose filling for tacos, enchiladas, and tostadas.

   1 pound lean ground beef
      Salad oil or lard (optional)
   1 medium-size onion, chopped
   ½ cup Mexican red chile sauce (page 62 or
      canned) or canned enchilada sauce

In a wide frying pan over medium-high heat, crumble and brown ground beef, adding salad oil if needed. Add onion and cook until limp. Moisten with Mexican chile sauce. Cover and simmer for 10 minutes, stirring occasionally, to blend flavors. Makes about 3 cups.

Picadillo Filling

(pee-kah-*dee*-yoh)

This filling, a spiced ground beef and sausage mixture with the sweet mellow addition of raisins, can be wrapped in warm corn tortillas and eaten out of hand.

   ¼ pound chorizo (purchased), skinned, or ½ cup
      bulk chorizo (recipe follows)
   1 pound lean ground beef
   1 medium-size onion, chopped
   ¼ teaspoon ground cinnamon
   ¼ cup raisins
   1 can (4½ oz.) chopped ripe olives
   ½ cup *each* catsup and water
   12 corn tortillas (page 74 or purchased)
      Garnishes: 1½ cups (about 6 oz.) shredded
         Cheddar cheese; 2 cups shredded lettuce; 1
         or 2 medium-size tomatoes, chopped; 1
         small package (3 oz.) cream cheese, cut in
         ½-inch cubes; ¾ to 1 cup guacamole (page 9
         or purchased)

In a wide frying pan over medium heat, crumble chorizo and ground beef. Add onion to pan along with cinnamon, and cook, stirring often, until meat begins to brown. Add raisins, olives, catsup, and water.

Simmer, uncovered, stirring occasionally, until most of the liquid is evaporated. Serve hot or chill and reheat, if made ahead.

Heat tortillas following directions for warm, soft, corn tortillas (page 74).

To serve, spoon portions of meat mixture onto center of warm tortillas. Garnish with shredded cheese, lettuce, tomatoes, chunks of cream cheese, and dollops of guacamole. Fold over to eat out of hand. Makes 4 to 6 servings.

Bulk Chorizo Filling

Rellenos Suelto de Chorizo
(rreh-*yeh*-nohs *suel*-toh deh cho-*ree*-soh)

The spicy chorizo sausage that is such a popular filling for tortilla dishes usually comes in link form. But in parts of Mexico and the Southwest you can also buy this sausage freshly ground in bulk form. With this recipe you can make your own similar chorizo mixture.

   1 large onion, finely chopped
   1 pound lean ground beef
   ½ pound lean ground pork
   2 teaspoons *each* chili powder and oregano
      leaves, crumbled
   ½ teaspoon ground cumin
   ¼ teaspoon ground cinnamon
   1 teaspoon salt
   ½ teaspoon liquid hot pepper seasoning
      (optional)
   5 tablespoons vinegar
   1½ cups canned enchilada sauce

Combine onion, ground beef, ground pork, chili powder, oregano, cumin, cinnamon, salt, hot pepper seasoning (if used), and vinegar.

In a wide frying pan over medium-high heat, brown meat mixture lightly, breaking it apart as it cooks. Add enchilada sauce and boil rapidly, uncovered, until liquid is gone. Skim off accumulated fat. Makes 3½ cups filling.

Pork or Chicken Filling

Relleno de Carne de Puerco o Pollo
rreh-*yeh*-noh deh kar-neh deh *puer*-koh oh *poh*-yoh)

The mild flavor of cooked pork or poultry combines well with both the sweetness of raisins and the spiciness of chiles.

   1 medium-size onion, chopped
   1½ tablespoons salad oil or lard
   2 cups finely diced or shredded, cooked lean
      pork, chicken, or turkey
   1 small canned jalapeño chile or other pickled,
      very hot chile, minced
   ¼ cup raisins
   1½ tablespoons chopped ripe olives
   ⅔ cup Mexican red chile sauce (page 62 or
      canned) or canned enchilada sauce

In a wide frying pan over medium-high heat, cook onion in oil until limp. Stir in meat, chile, raisins, olives, and chile sauce. Simmer, uncovered, for 10 minutes, stirring occasionally, to blend flavors. Makes 2½ to 3 cups.

Vegetables, Beans, and Rice

Dishes to go with any meal

Refried beans, Spanish rice, and corn come to mind when one thinks of Mexican vegetables. While beans are far and away the most popular vegetable in Mexico, rice and corn are also favorites.

These and other vegetables are seldom served alone in Mexico. Usually they are worked into other dishes for flavor, color, or texture. When cooked and served as a "vegetable dish," they are embellished with sauce, cheese, meat, seasonings, or garnish (they need not be highly spiced or seasoned). Enchiladas, tostadas, and tacos make good use of a variety of vegetables treated in these ways.

Sometimes several kinds of vegetables are combined for a dish. Baked corn pudding joins red and green pepper with onion and corn; calabacita blends zucchini with corn and peppers; even eggplant is enhanced with mushrooms.

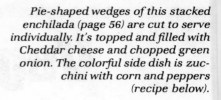

Pie-shaped wedges of this stacked enchilada (page 56) are cut to serve individually. It's topped and filled with Cheddar cheese and chopped green onion. The colorful side dish is zucchini with corn and peppers (recipe below).

Baked Corn Pudding

Pudin de Elote
(poo-*theen* deh *loh*-teh)

Sweet corn pudding can be made ahead, then baked an hour before serving.

- **6 tablespoons butter or margarine**
- **1 large onion, chopped**
- **1 clove garlic, minced or pressed**
- **1 *each* medium-size red and green bell pepper, seeded and chopped**
- **⅓ cup all-purpose flour, unsifted**
- **1 teaspoon salt**
- **1 tablespoon sugar**
- **¼ teaspoon pepper**
- **2 cans (16 oz. *each*) cream-style corn**
- **6 eggs, slightly beaten**
- **2 cups milk**

Melt butter in a 5-quart kettle over medium heat; add onion, garlic, and bell peppers. Cook, stirring, until onion is limp. Stir in flour, salt, sugar, and pepper; cook, stirring, until bubbly. Remove from heat; add corn, eggs, and milk, stirring until mixture is well blended.

Pour corn mixture into shallow, buttered 3-quart baking dish. (Cover and refrigerate as long as 24 hours.) Bake in a 350° oven for 55 minutes or until center appears set when dish is gently shaken. (If chilled, bake 1 hour and 5 minutes.) Makes about 10 servings.

Zucchini with Corn & Peppers

Calabacita
(ka-lah-bah-*see*-tah)

A bright addition to any meal, red, green, and yellow vegetables are flavored with garlic. (See photograph at right.)

- **3 tablespoons bacon drippings, butter, or margarine**
- **2½ pounds zucchini, cut into ½-inch cubes**
- **About 1½ cups freshly cut corn (from 3 or 4 medium-size ears), or 1 package (10 oz.) frozen corn, thawed**
- **1 red or green bell pepper, seeded and chopped**
- **1 medium-size onion, chopped**
- **2 cloves garlic, minced or pressed**
- **Salt and pepper**

In a wide frying pan over high heat, melt bacon drippings. Add zucchini, corn, bell pepper, onion, and garlic; cook, stirring often, until most vegetable liquid has evaporated and vegetables are tender-crisp (about 5 minutes). Add salt and pepper to taste. Makes 8 to 10 servings.

Carrots in Milk

Zanahorias en Leche
(sah-nah-*oh*-reas en *leh*-cheh)

Carrots baked in milk with a garnish of minced parsley, Guadalajara-style, can dress up a family meal or lend balance to a menu of spicy dishes.

- **8 large carrots, very thinly sliced**
- **1 cup milk**
- **1 teaspoon sugar**
- **1 teaspoon salt**
- **½ teaspoon pepper**
- **2 tablespoons butter or margarine**
- **2 tablespoons minced parsley**

Place carrots in a buttered 1½-quart baking dish. Mix together milk, sugar, salt, and pepper; pour over carrots. Dot with butter.

Cover tightly and cook in a 350° oven for about 1 hour or until carrots are fork tender. Sprinkle parsley evenly over top and serve immediately. Makes about 6 servings.

Lemon Green Beans

Ejotes con Limon
(e-*hoh*-tehs kohn lee-*mohn*)

Citrus juice often is the only touch that makes a dish "Mexican." In Guadalajara cooks prepare green beans with a simple parsley-butter sauce, then give it that typical finish—the juice of a fresh lemon.

- **1½ pounds green beans, cut in 1½-inch lengths, or 2 packages (10 oz. *each*) frozen cut green beans**
- **Boiling salted water**
- **3 tablespoons butter or margarine, melted**
- **½ teaspoon salt**
- **¼ teaspoon pepper**
- **1 tablespoon minced parsley**
- **2 to 3 tablespoons lemon juice**

(Continued on page 68)

 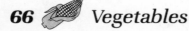

Cook beans, uncovered, in boiling salted water to cover until tender-crisp (or follow package directions). Drain and place in serving dish. Mix together butter, salt, pepper, parsley, and lemon juice; pour over beans. Serve hot. Makes about 6 servings.

Fried Bananas

Platanos Fritos
(*plah*-tah-nohs *free*-tohs)

Bananas are often served as a vegetable with simple roasted or broiled meats and fowl the Mexicans so frequently eat.

To increase the number of servings, simply double or triple both ingredients.

1 firm, green-tipped banana
1½ teaspoons butter or margarine

Peel banana and cut in half lengthwise. In a wide frying pan over medium-low heat, melt butter. Place banana, cut side down, in butter and cook over medium-low heat for about 10 minutes or until lightly browned. Carefully turn bananas and cook another 5 to 7 minutes or until lightly browned. Serve warm. Makes 1 or 2 servings.

Refried Beans

Frijoles Refritos
(free-*hoh*-less rrreh-*free*-tohs)

The secret of the best refried beans is ample use of fat. Even canned beans can be improved by additional cooking with flavorful fat.

The name "refried" should not be taken literally to mean "fried again." In Spanish "re" sometimes means "very" or "thoroughly." One frying is enough, if it is a thorough one.

Refried beans go into so many Mexican dishes because they are economical, delicious, and nutritious, and they keep well when refrigerated. (See cover photograph and page 70.)

1 pound dried pinto or pink beans
About 5 cups water
1 or 2 medium-size onions, diced (optional)
½ to 1 cup hot bacon drippings, butter, margarine, or lard
Salt

Thoroughly wash and drain beans; discard any foreign material. Combine beans in a 3-quart pan with water and onions. Soak in cold water overnight or bring to a boil, cover, and remove from heat for 1 hour.

Return to heat, bring to a boil, then cover and simmer (adding more water, if needed) until beans are very tender and mash readily (about 3 hours). Drain and mash beans with potato masher or electric mixer, adding bacon drippings. Mix well; continue cooking, stirring frequently, until beans are thickened and fat is absorbed. Add salt to taste. Serve hot or reheat. Makes 6 to 8 side-dish servings or 5 to 6 cups.

Oaxacan Baked Black Beans

Frijoles Negros a la Oaxaca
(free-*hoh*-less *neh*-grohs ah lah ooa-*hah*-ka)

You'll need to plan ahead to make this dish from the south-coast state of Oaxaca—the small, black-skinned, dried beans should bake for about 10 hours. Substitute pinto beans if you can't find black ones. Some markets, especially those stocking many gourmet foods, do have black beans. Or try Oriental or health food stores. (See photograph on page 46.)

2 pounds dried black or pinto beans
12 cups water
2 cloves garlic, minced or pressed
1 medium-size onion, chopped
1½ teaspoons cumin seed
  About 2 pounds lean ham hocks trimmed of excess fat
  Salt
¼ teaspoon pepper

Thoroughly wash and drain beans; discard any foreign material. Place beans in a 5-quart baking dish. Cover with water; add garlic, onion, cumin seed, ham hocks, 1 teaspoon salt, and pepper.

Cover and bake in a 275° oven for about 10 hours or until beans are tender and mash readily. (You can cook the beans overnight or start the day before, refrigerate overnight, and start again in the morning.)

Skim off as much fat as possible before serving, and add more salt to taste, if needed. Makes 8 to 12 generous servings.

Sautéed Green Peppers

Chiles Verdes Fritos
(*chee*-lehs *ver*-dehs *free*-tohs)

Green bell peppers, sautéed just until they begin to lose their crispness, make a colorful accompaniment for roasted or barbecued beef, lamb, or pork.

1 tablespoon butter or margarine
4 green bell peppers, seeded and cut into thin
strips

In a wide frying pan over high heat, melt butter. Add peppers and cook, stirring frequently, for about 5 minutes or until peppers are bright green and just beginning to lose their crispness. Serve at once. Makes 4 servings.

Eggplant Acapulco

Berenjena a la Acapulco
(beh-ren-*heh*-nah a lah ah-kah-*pool*-koh)

Mushrooms and Romano cheese make this an out-of-the-ordinary eggplant dish. It's a good choice for a buffet dinner.

1 large eggplant
Boiling salted water
½ cup fine dry bread crumbs
½ cup grated Romano or Parmesan cheese
¼ cup butter or margarine
Salt and pepper
½ pound mushrooms, sliced
2 cans (8 oz. *each*) tomato sauce

Place whole, unpeeled eggplant in about 4 inches boiling salted water (eggplant floats); reduce heat and simmer, uncovered, for 10 minutes. Drain and allow to cool enough to handle. Cut it into quarters lengthwise; peel each quarter, then cut crosswise into 1-inch pieces; set aside. Mix bread crumbs with cheese.

In a buttered 2-quart baking dish, arrange half the eggplant pieces. Dot with half the butter. Sprinkle lightly with salt and pepper to taste. Add half the mushrooms, tomato sauce, and crumb mixture. Repeat layers. Bake, uncovered, in a 350° oven for 45

minutes or until eggplant is fork tender. Serve hot. Makes 6 servings.

White Rice

Arroz Blanco (ah-*rrros blahn*-koh)

Arroz blanco is similar to rice pilaf. Rice is toasted slowly in oil to give flavor and every grain comes out separate and fluffy.

1½ cups rice
¼ cup salad oil
1 clove garlic
1 medium-size white onion, chopped
2 chicken bouillon cubes
3 cups boiling water
Salt

In a wide frying pan, place rice, oil, garlic, and onion. Slowly brown rice over low heat, stirring occasionally. When rice is wheat colored, pour off most of the oil (leave about 1 tablespoon) and remove garlic.

Dissolve bouillon cubes in water and pour over rice. Simmer, covered, until liquid is absorbed (about 20 minutes). Add salt to taste. Makes about 6 servings.

Tortilla "Dry Soup"

Sopa Seca de Tortillas
(*soh*-pah *seh*-kah deh tor-*tee* yahs)

Because this spicy casserole, rich with cheese, contains strips of tortillas, it might also be classified with chilaquiles (page 39).

1 cup minced onion
2 tablespoons salad oil, lard, or shortening
4 canned California green chiles (seeds and pith removed), minced
1 cup whipping cream
1 cup tomato purée
Salt
12 corn tortillas (page 74 or purchased), cut in thin strips and fried (page 77)
2 cups (about 8 oz.) shredded jack cheese
2 tablespoons butter or margarine

In a wide frying pan, over medium-high heat, cook onion in oil until limp; add chiles, cream, and tomato purée. Simmer 10 minutes. Add salt to taste.

Grease a 2-quart baking dish and cover bottom with half the tortilla strips. Pour over half the sauce and add half the shredded cheese. Repeat layers, ending with cheese. Dot with butter and bake, uncovered, in a 350° oven for 30 minutes or until hot through. Makes 6 servings.

Colossal chicken tamales (page 52), steamed in their own corn husk wrappers, are larger than typical Mexican tamales. Top with green taco sauce. Mexican vegetable rice is studded with shredded carrot and peas (recipe below). Refried beans (page 68) complete meal.

Rice "Dry Soup"

Sopa Seca de Arroz
(*soh*-pah *seh*-kah deh ah-*rros*)

Better known as Spanish rice, this tomato-flavored rice is often served alongside refried beans in Mexican restaurants in the United States. At fiesta or full-course meals, both a regular soup and a sopa seca or "dry soup" are included. This is dry in the sense that whatever liquid is used during the cooking is completely absorbed into the filling foundation, usually something starchy, such as rice, pasta, tortillas, or dried legumes.

The variations which follow contain meat, seafood, or eggs and can be served as entrées as well as accompaniments.

- **2 cups rice**
- **6 tablespoons lard, butter, or margarine**
- **2 small onions, finely chopped**
- **2 cloves garlic, minced or pressed**
- **4 medium-size tomatoes, peeled and chopped, or 1 cup tomato purée**
- **About 4 cups regular-strength beef or chicken broth**
- **2 or 3 canned California green chiles, or fresh green chiles, seeded and chopped (optional)**
- **2 tablespoons chopped fresh coriander (cilantro), optional**
- **1 cup pimento-stuffed green olives**

In a wide frying pan over medium-high heat, brown rice lightly in lard. Add onion, garlic, and tomato, and cook for 2 or 3 minutes; add 3 cups of the broth and chiles, if used.

Cover and simmer 25 to 35 minutes or bake, covered, in a 350° oven 50 to 60 minutes. Add more broth, if needed, to cook rice. However, there should be no liquid remaining when rice is tender to bite. Add coriander, if desired, during last 10 minutes. Garnish rice with olives. Makes 6 servings.

Rice "Dry Soup" & Shrimp

Sopa de Arroz con Camaron
(*soh*-pah deh ar-*rros* kohn kah-mah-*ron*)

Follow directions above for rice "dry soup."

Add 1 pound cooked, shelled, deveined **shrimp** 5 minutes before **rice** is finished cooking; heat through. Makes 6 servings.

Rice "Dry Soup" with Peas & Ham

Sopa de Arroz con Chicharos y Jamon
(*soh*-pah deh ah-*rros* kohn *chee*-chah-ros ee hah-*mohn*)

Follow directions at left for rice "dry soup."

Add 1 pound diced cooked **ham** when adding **broth**. About 10 minutes before **rice** is finished cooking, add 2 cups frozen **peas**, thawed. Makes 6 servings.

Rice "Dry Soup" with Eggs

Sopa de Arroz con Huevos
(*soh*-pah deh ah-*rros* kohn *weh*-vohs)

Follow directions at left for rice "dry soup."

About 10 minutes before **rice** finishes cooking, make six depressions in top of rice with back of tablespoon. Drop 1 raw **egg** into each depression, sprinkle eggs generously with grated **Parmesan cheese**, and continue cooking, covered, until eggs are set. Makes 6 servings.

Mexican Vegetable Rice

Arroz con Legumbres Mexicano
(ah-*rros* kohn leh-*goom*-bres meh-hee-*ka*-noh)

One package of frozen peas and carrots stirred into garlic-flavored rice makes a colorful side dish. Stir in tomatoes just before serving. (See photograph at left.)

- **3 tablespoons salad oil**
- **1 large onion, chopped**
- **2 cloves garlic, minced or pressed**
- **1½ cups rice**
- **½ teaspoon salt**
- **⅛ teaspoon cayenne**
- **3 chicken bouillon cubes**
- **3 cups boiling water**
- **1 package (10 oz.) frozen mixed peas and carrots (thawed)**
- **1½ cups peeled, seeded, and chopped tomatoes**

In a wide frying pan, heat oil over medium heat; add onion, garlic, and rice. Cook, stirring, until onion is limp and rice is opaque. Stir in salt, cayenne, and bouillon cubes dissolved in boiling water; bring to boil, cover, and simmer for 20 minutes or until liquid is absorbed.

Add peas and carrots and tomatoes. Cook over low heat, stirring just until vegetables are heated through (about 3 minutes). Makes 8 to 10 servings.

 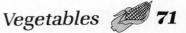

Tortillas and Breads

Wheat and corn staples

Tortillas are, of course, *the* bread of Mexico. This chapter tells you how to make tortillas and how to serve them.

Both corn and flour tortillas are frequently served as bread in a soft, steamy-hot form (often folded and wrapped in a napkin which helps keep them warm as long as possible). To prepare hot, soft tortillas, see instructions on page 76.

Crisp-fried tortillas, whole ones or wedges, are another popular bread form. Frying instructions are on page 76.

Other favorite breads range from plain wheat loaves or crusty rolls, such as the bolillo, which is an oval, pointed, French-type roll, to rolls that have a bland flavor and porous texture or are puffy and flaky. These are formed into a myriad of fanciful shapes and given fanciful or funny names.

Some of the breads are sweet, perhaps studded with fruits and nuts. They may be enjoyed as a coffee cake or dessert, accompanied with Mexican hot chocolate.

Other kinds are deep-fried such as sopapillas, which come out of the hot fat puffy and crunchy (page 77).

 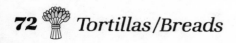

Tortillas

(tor-*tee*-yahs)

When the ancient Mexicans invented tortillas—their flat, round, unleavened bread—they invented the most versatile bread of all. It can be stacked, rolled, folded, torn, cut, and crumbled; it tastes good soft and hot, crisp-fried, or toasted. It can be shaped with the hands and easily baked on an improvised griddle over any source of heat; it keeps well, and can be reheated later.

Mexicans substitute tortillas for eating utensils by using them as a scoop, or as a plate when laid in the palm of the hand and filled with food.

The tortilla is a food born out of the necessities of primitive people. The first ones were made of the native corn, dried to keep until the next crop came in. The kernels were simmered in water with lime until partially soft (this is called "nixtamal"), then laboriously ground by hand on a stone mortar called a "metate." The moist meal, called "masa," was patted into a thin pancake and baked on a "comal" (a clay griddle).

When the Spaniards introduced wheat flour, cooks quickly used it for tortillas, too. However, the flour tortillas never became as widely used, and now they are more a specialty of the northern part of the country.

Today the ways of preparing tortillas have changed somewhat in the more urban areas. Machines may grind the corn and wheat, and occasionally machines may shape, bake, and even freeze the product. The moist masa sometimes is dehydrated and sold in bags like flour, later to be mixed with water at home.

In the United States, taco stands and supermarkets peddle the tortilla and hostesses serve purchased tortilla chips to scoop up cocktail dips.

But the corn tortilla made most places in modern Mexico is little different from what the Mexican Indians made hundreds of years ago. In the market places, you will see women working huge white mounds of masa, which oozes excess liquid, until the dough has just the right feel. Then they slap and pat it into cakes and bake them on the spot.

The slap-slap sounds of many tortilla-makers at work and the heady scent of cooking corn are sensuous experiences of the real Mexico which many visitors long remember.

Tortillas are so basic to Mexican cookery that an understanding of how to buy, make, and cook them will provide greater success for anyone preparing recipes from this book.

All the recipes in this book specify whether corn or flour tortillas should be used.

How to Buy Tortillas

In most food stores in the West, both corn and flour tortillas are sold, usually by the dozen in a plastic-wrapped package (or sometimes in a box or can). They may be found in the refrigerated area of the store, in a freezer, or on a shelf, if canned.

Corn tortillas are usually 6 inches in diameter; flour tortillas are 7 inches or much larger.

Frozen tortillas keep almost indefinitely under ideal freezing temperature (0° or colder), but do lose their flavor and moisture within a matter of weeks in refrigerator freezing compartments at higher temperatures. Those that aren't frozen may be kept refrigerated for several days, or frozen at home for somewhat longer storage.

Thaw frozen tortillas before reheating by separating them, brushing off ice crystals, and laying them flat. They will thaw in about 5 minutes; if you don't use them right away, cover with foil or plastic film to keep from drying out.

The quality of tortillas you buy can vary considerably. If you want the best cooking results, compare the brands available to you. If you buy unfrozen tortillas, be sure they are fresh. Bend the package to see that the bread is still tender and flexible; it should not look dry around the edges.

The tortillas you buy have already been cooked. But to serve them as bread or to use them in cooking, you will need to reheat or fry them.

How to Make Tortillas

If you live in an area where ready-made tortillas are not sold, or if you want the pleasure and superior results of making your own, recipes are provided in this chapter for making both the corn and flour types.

Flour tortillas can be made from the regular all-purpose flour you have on hand, but corn tortillas require the special corn preparation called masa harina (dehydrated masa flour), if you do not have access to fresh masa. Don't try to make tortillas with regular corn meal, which is too coarsely ground and prepared differently from the corn for masa.

Masa harina is sold in 5-pound (or larger) bags at stores specializing in Mexican or gourmet foods. Since it is also used for tamales and other specialties and keeps like flour, it would be wise to buy an ample supply when you locate a source.

Both flour and corn tortillas can be patted into shape by hand, but the technique is something best learned at a Mexican mother's knee. Lacking such upbringing, you may roll the dough with a rolling pin, trimming each tortilla to an even round if you wish. For quickest and best results, you may want to invest in an inexpensive tortilla press or even make one according to the instructions following.

 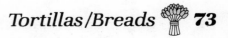

Homemade Tortilla Press

A tortilla press that works well can be easily made from a few scraps of lumber. And the rougher your woodworking, the more authentic it looks. *See diagram below.*

Use any 3/4 to 1-inch-thick wood on hand, choosing unwarped boards that will fit together evenly. Cut the paddle-shaped bottom from an 8½ by 12½-inch piece, leaving a handle on one end where you attach the 2 by 2-inch pressure arm. Glue and nail four 1 by 2 crosspieces to the top and bottom boards to help prevent warping when the press is washed. Attach hinges securely with long screws.

Last, locate the arm's 1/4-inch bolt at a height where the arm can lever down (not completely horizontally) over the top of the press.

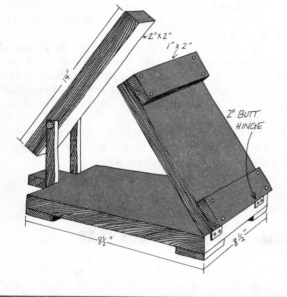

farthest from handle. Flatten it slightly with the palm of your hand. Cover with a second square of waxed paper. Lower top half of press (being careful not to wrinkle paper), and press down firmly on lever until the tortilla measures about 6 inches in diameter (4 inches for small tortillas). Stack paper-covered dough and cook according to instructions that follow.

Rolling pin method of shaping. Use two cloths which have been dipped in water and wrung dry. Flatten a ball of dough slightly and place between the cloths. Roll with light, even strokes until cake is about 6 inches in diameter. Carefully pull back cloths, trim tortilla to a round shape if necessary, and sandwich it between two squares of waxed paper. Roll out all remaining dough balls similarly. Cook according to instructions that follow.

Cooking instructions. Peel off top piece of waxed paper carefully. Turn over tortilla, paper side up, onto a preheated, ungreased, medium-hot griddle, or into a heavy frying pan over medium-high heat. As tortilla becomes warm, you will be able to peel off remaining paper.

Bake for about 1½ to 2 minutes, turning frequently, until tortilla looks dry (it should be soft) and is lightly flecked with brown specks. (It will puff up briefly.)

Serve tortillas immediately while still warm, or cool and wrap airtight. Store airtight packages in refrigerator or freezer. To serve, reheat or fry (follow directions, page 76). Makes 1 dozen 6-inch or 2 dozen 4-inch corn tortillas.

Corn Tortillas

Tortillas de Maiz (tor-*tee*-yahs deh mah-*ees*)

Flat, 6-inch round corn tortillas are the most versatile Mexican "bread." They can be eaten immediately or stored in refrigerator or freezer until needed. (See photograph of golden corn tortillas at right.)

2 cups masa harina (dehydrated masa flour)
1¼ to 1⅓ cups warm water

Mix masa flour with enough warm water to make dough hold together well. Using your hands, shape dough into a smooth ball. Divide dough into 12 equal pieces, then roll each into a ball. (For small tortillas, divide dough into 24 equal pieces.)

Tortilla press method of shaping. Place a square of waxed paper on bottom half of tortilla press; place 1 ball of dough on paper, slightly off center toward edge

Flour Tortillas

Tortillas de Harina (tor-*tee*-yahs deh ah-*ree*-nah)

Generally larger than corn tortillas, flour tortillas offer a more mellow foundation for the Mexican dishes that are seasoned more subtly. (See photograph of white flour tortillas at right.)

3 cups all-purpose flour, unsifted
2 teaspoons baking powder
¾ teaspoon salt
About 1 cup warm water

Stir together flour, baking powder and salt. Gradually stir in enough warm water to form a crumbly dough; then work dough with your hands until it holds together. Turn out onto a board and knead until smooth. Divide into 12 pieces and shape each into a smooth ball. Cover lightly with plastic film and let rest about 15 minutes.

For each tortilla, flatten one ball into a 4 or 5-inch patty, then roll into about a 9-inch round, rolling from

 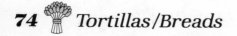

center to edges. Turn tortilla often, stretching dough as you carefully peel it off board.

As each tortilla is shaped, place on preheated, dry, heavy griddle or heavy wide frying pan over medium-high heat. On a preheated electric griddle set at medium-high heat or about 375°.

Almost immediately, tiny blisters should appear. Turn tortilla and immediately start pressing a wide spatula directly on top of it—press gently but firmly all over the top. Blisters will form over most of surface as you press. Turn tortilla and press all over other side until blisters turn a golden brown; tortilla should remain soft. If tortillas stick or brown too quickly, reduce heat.

Stack tortillas as cooked inside a folded cloth towel within a plastic bag; close bag and let tortillas steam and soften until all are cooked.

Serve tortillas as soon as they are soft; or cool, remove from bag, wrap in foil, and refrigerate or freeze. Makes 1 dozen 9-inch flour tortillas.

Reheating, Softening, & Frying Tortillas

With any Mexican meal, serve whole, plain tortillas (corn or flour) as a bread. These are usually served soft and hot, preferably wrapped in a napkin to keep them moist and warm as long as possible. Both the tortillas you make from scratch and those you buy can be prepared this way quickly if you follow directions carefully.

Instructions follow for preparing soft, hot tortillas on an ungreased surface or in a conventional or microwave oven. Sometimes they are buttered before serving and folded or rolled to keep the melted butter inside. Extra butter may be served at the table, or just provide butter for those who want it.

Corn tortillas provide a cracker-type accompaniment when crisp-fried in oil (instructions follow). They can be fried whole but are most convenient to serve if they are cut into wedges before cooking. These wedges can serve as dippers for guacamole and other appetizers and as an accompaniment for soups or salads. They are best hot but are also palatable cold and will keep their crispness for several hours unwrapped.

Crisp-fried tortillas are called tostadas, which means "toasted." Tostada also is the name of a stacked salad (page 23) with a crisp tortilla as a base, piled high with meat, beans, shredded lettuce, and cheese. To avoid confusion, the recipes in this book will refer to the plain, fried tortillas cut in wedges as "tortilla chips." (The Mexicans sometimes call them by the diminutive, "tostaditas," which would be the least confusing term if consistently used.)

How to reheat and soften corn or flour tortillas. Fresh tortillas are already soft in a sense, but when reheated they become even more tender and flexible. If tortillas are dry and a little hard, dip your hand in water and rub it lightly onto surfaces of the bread before heating. Be sure not to heat tortillas longer than necessary to soften and warm them thoroughly, or they will become hard and brittle.

On an ungreased surface. Place tortillas so they do not overlap on a medium-hot griddle or in a heavy frying pan over medium-high heat. Turn *frequently* until soft and hot (about 30 seconds on each side).

Put immediately into a covered ovenproof container or foil packet; then hold in a 200° oven until all tortillas are heated. (The secret is to keep them from drying out once heated.)

In a conventional oven. Stack tortillas, wrap in foil, and place in a 350° oven until hot and steamy (about 15 minutes).

In microwave oven. Stack tortillas, wrap in plastic film (or puncture several holes in plastic package of purchased tortillas), and cook until hot and steamy (1 to 1½ minutes for 12 tortillas).

How to keep soft tortillas hot several hours. Wrap hot tortillas airtight in foil and place in an insulated bag, or wrap the foil package in a cloth and then 12 or 14 sheets of newspaper. The tortillas will stay hot for at least 2 hours in the paper wrapping, and longer than that in the insulated bag. You can use this method for picnics or any occasion when it would be handy to prepare tortillas ahead of time.

How to toast corn or flour tortillas. Place tortillas on a grill or in a hinged broiler 3 or 4 inches above a low flame or coals; cook, turning frequently with a fork or tongs, until tortillas are heated through, soft, and lightly blistered (about 1 minute).

How to crisp-fry whole corn or flour tortillas. Heat 1/2 inch salad oil, shortening, or lard in a wide frying pan over medium-high heat to 350° on a deep-fat frying thermometer. Fry one tortilla at a time, using a spatula or tongs to turn tortilla frequently or to hold it

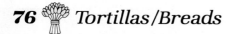

under fat until it crisps, puffs slightly, and browns lightly (about 1 minute or less). Drain on paper towels.

How to crisp-fry corn tortilla chips or strips (tostadas or tostaditas). Cut tortillas into pie-shaped wedges (4ths, 6ths, or 8ths) or thin strips. Heat about 1 inch of salad oil, shortening, or lard in a wide frying pan over medium-high heat to 350° on a deep-fat frying thermometer. Fry just a few at a time, turning occasionally, until crisp and lightly browned (about 1 minute or less). Drain on paper towels; sprinkle lightly with salt if desired. Store airtight.

Hard Rolls

Bolillos
(boh-*lee*-yohs)

Bolillos have a crisp outer crust similar to hard French rolls and are soft inside. For maximum flavor and freshness, serve them still warm from the oven with plenty of butter. The rolls regain their crispness when reheated, and are a special breakfast treat served with jam or jelly. To reheat, place them directly on the racks of a 350° oven for 15 to 20 minutes.

Use bolillos in place of sliced bread or dinner rolls. They can be split in half for cold sandwiches, or served as a bread accompaniment with salads or bowls of soup or stew. (See photograph on page 78.)

```
  2 cups water
1½ tablespoons sugar
  1 tablespoon salt
  2 tablespoons butter or margarine
  1 package active dry yeast
    About 6 cups all-purpose flour, unsifted
  1 teaspoon cornstarch dissolved in ½ cup water
```

In a pan combine water, sugar, salt, and butter. Warm over low heat, stirring, to a temperature between 105° and 115° on a candy thermometer. Pour into a large bowl; stir in yeast until dissolved. With an electric mixer or heavy spoon, beat in 5 cups of the flour to form a dough.

Turn dough onto a board coated with about 1/2 cup of the remaining flour and knead for 10 minutes or until dough is smooth and feels velvety; add more flour if needed to keep dough from sticking. Place in a greased bowl and turn dough over to grease top. Cover bowl with clear plastic film and let rise in a warm place until dough has almost doubled (about 1½ hours).

Punch down and squeeze dough to release air bubbles, then turn out onto a lightly floured board. Divide into 16 equal pieces. Form each piece into a smooth ball. Shape each into an oblong by rolling it and gently pulling from the center to the ends until it is about 4 inches long (center should be thicker than ends). Place rolls about 2 inches apart on greased baking sheets. Cover lightly with a towel.

Let rolls rise for about 35 minutes or until they are almost doubled in size.

In a pan, heat cornstarch and water to boiling; cool slightly. Brush each roll with cornstarch mixture; then, with a sharp knife or razor blade, cut a slash about 3/4 inch deep and about 2 inches long on top of each roll.

Bake in a 375° oven for 35 to 40 minutes or until they are golden brown and sound hollow when tapped. Cool on wire racks and wrap tightly to store. Makes 16 rolls.

Puffy Fried Bread

Sopapillas
(soh-pa-*pee*-yas)

In Mexico a favored sweet snack is sopapillas, a fried pastry that is comparable to our doughnuts. This especially easy version makes use of frozen yeast bread dough. The hot bits may be eaten when first cooked or rewarmed; you dip each bite in heated honey and butter.

Thaw 1-pound loaf of **frozen wheat or white bread dough**. Heat 1 or 2 inches **salad oil** in small pan to 375° on a deep-fat frying thermometer. Tear off lumps of dough 3/4 inch in diameter; stretch thin and drop into oil.

Cook, turning, about 1½ minutes or until sopapillas are well browned; drain on paper towels. Serve hot or reheat on baking sheet in a 375° oven for about 5 minutes. Dip each bite in a mixture of 1/2 cup **honey** heated with 3 tablespoons **butter** or margarine. Makes about 60 sopapillas.

Mexican Cornbread

Pan de Mais (pahn deh mah-*ees*)

Mild California green chiles give character to cornbread . . . add them to suit your mood.

```
  2 eggs
¼ cup salad oil
  1 to 4 canned California green chiles, seeded
      and chopped
  1 small can (about 9 oz.) cream-style corn
½ cup sour cream
  1 cup yellow cornmeal
½ teaspoon salt
  2 teaspoons baking powder
  2 cups (about 8 oz.) shredded sharp Cheddar
      cheese
```

(Continued on page 79)

Fanciful Mexican breads make a colorful array. From back, clockwise: maraschino cherry-studded three kings' bread (page 80), football-shaped bolillos (page 77), Mexican sweet buns in various shapes (recipe below), and in center, pan de muerto with its crossbones (recipe below).

... *Mexican Cornbread (cont'd.)*

In a large bowl, beat eggs and salad oil until well blended. Add chiles to egg mixture. Then add corn, sour cream, cornmeal, salt, baking powder, and 1½ cups of the cheese; stir until thoroughly blended. Pour into a greased 8 or 9-inch round or square pan. Sprinkle remaining 1/2 cup cheese evenly over top. Bake in a 350° oven for 1 hour or until wooden pick inserted in the center comes out clean and crust is lightly browned.

Serve warm; or cool completely, wrap in heavy foil, and refrigerate or freeze. Reheat (wrapped in foil) in a 300° oven. If chilled, heat 30 minutes; if frozen, 1 hour. Makes 6 to 8 servings.

Mexican Sweet Buns

Pan Dulce (pahn *dool*-seh)

South-of-the-border bakers have a talent for creating fanciful designs. In their hands a simple ball of dough quickly becomes a seashell, a horn, or other imaginative shape. Fill or top each bun with a generous portion of buttery streusel mixture, plain or chocolate. (See photograph at left.)

    1 cup milk
    6 tablespoons butter or margarine
    1 package active dry yeast
    1 teaspoon salt
    ⅓ cup sugar
      About 5 cups all-purpose flour, unsifted
    2 eggs
      Plain and chocolate egg streusel (recipes
        follow)
    1 egg beaten with 2 tablespoons milk

Heat the 1 cup milk and butter (cut into chunks) in a pan until very warm (120° to 130° on a candy thermometer); butter need not melt completely. In large bowl of an electric mixer, combine yeast, salt, sugar, and 2 cups of the flour. Pour in milk mixture and beat on medium speed for 2 minutes; scrape bowl often. Blend in eggs and 1 cup more flour; beat on high speed for 2 minutes. Gradually beat in enough of the remaining flour (about 1½ cups) to form a stiff dough, using a spoon or a heavy-duty mixer on low to medium speed.

Turn dough out on a floured board and knead until smooth and elastic (about 5 minutes). Turn dough over in a greased bowl, cover, and let rise in a warm place until doubled (about 1½ hours).

Prepare both plain and chocolate egg streusel.

Punch down dough and turn out onto a floured board. Divide into 14 equal pieces and shape each into a smooth ball.

Make 7 of the dough balls into shell shapes by patting into 3-inch rounds. Top with 1/4 cup streusel rolled to a smooth layer, slashed, or piled in lumps.

Make 7 horn shapes by rolling each remaining ball to a 4 by 8-inch oval. Top with 3 tablespoons streusel. Roll from one end; stop halfway and fold in sides; then finish rolling and curl the ends.

To make corn ear shapes instead of horns, roll dough to a 4 by 8-inch oval. Top with 3 tablespoons streusel, then roll up from one end to the other, pulling ends out as you go. Cut slashes on top.

Place buns about 2 inches apart on greased baking sheets, placing streusel-topped buns on one sheet and the filled, plain-topped buns on another; lightly cover only the plain buns. Place buns in a warm place and let rise to almost double (about 45 minutes). Brush plain-topped buns with egg-milk mixture.

Bake buns in a 375° oven until tops are lightly browned (about 17 to 20 minutes). Serve warm; or cool on racks and wrap. To reheat, place, uncovered, in a 350° oven for about 12 minutes. Makes 14 buns.

Plain egg streusel. In a bowl, mix 1/2 cup **sugar** with 2/3 cup all-purpose **flour**, unsifted. Cut in 3½ tablespoons **butter** or margarine with a pastry blender, or by rubbing mixture between your fingers until fine, even crumbs form. With a fork, stir in 2 **egg yolks** until well blended. Lightly pack streusel in cup or spoon when measuring amount for buns.

Chocolate egg streusel. Prepare same as for plain egg streusel preceding, except add 2 tablespoons **ground chocolate** to sugar and flour.

Pan de Muertos

(pahn deh *muer*-tohs)
Bread of the Dead

Mexico's Day of the Dead, November 2, is a celebration of much merriment despite its name and the macabre design of the refreshments. One of the most famous of the traditional dishes is *pan de muerto*, or "bread of the dead," characterized by "bones" crossed on the surface. It's a simple yeast bread and fun to offer on our own Halloween. (See photograph at left.)

    ¼ cup milk
    ¼ cup butter or margarine, cut in small pieces
    ¼ cup sugar
    ½ teaspoon salt
    1 package active dry yeast
    ¼ cup warm water (about 110°)
    2 eggs
      About 3 cups all-purpose flour, unsifted
    ¼ teaspoon ground cinnamon
    2 teaspoons sugar
      Butter or margarine

(Continued on next page)

Bring milk to scalding; remove from heat and stir in butter, the 1/4 cup sugar, and salt. Let cool.

In a mixer bowl, combine yeast and water; let stand about 5 minutes; then add milk mixture. Separate 1 egg. Add yolk to yeast mixture (reserve white). Add remaining egg and 2⅓ cups of the flour; blend well.

Place dough on a well floured board and knead until smooth and velvety (about 5 minutes). Place in a bowl, cover, and let rise in a warm place until double (about 1½ hours). Knead again on a floured board to expel air bubbles.

Cut off a 1/3-cup-size piece of dough; set aside. Divide remaining dough in 3 equal parts; shape each into a rope about 12 inches long. Braid ropes together, pressing ends to hold securely; place on a greased baking sheet and join ends firmly to make a wreath. Divide reserved dough in half; shape each portion into a "bone." Cross bones and place across entire top of wreath.

Cover lightly and let rise in warm place for about 30 minutes or until puffy looking. Brush gently with reserved egg white (slightly beaten). Mix cinnamon and the 2 teaspoons sugar, sprinkle onto loaf, avoiding the bones. Bake in a 350° oven for about 35 minutes or until richly browned. Serve warm, cut in wedges, with butter. Makes 1 loaf.

Three Kings' Bread

Rosca de los Reyes (rrros-kah deh lohs rrrehs-yehs)

It is customary to serve Rosca de los Reyes, "Kings' Ring," to celebrate Twelfth-Night, the 6th of January. The fruit-filled yeast bread is baked in a ring and garnished with "jewels" of candied fruits and nuts.

Traditionally, a tiny doll or lima bean is hidden inside the bread. The guest who receives the wedge with the doll is obliged to give another party on the coming February 2, a religious holiday called El Dia de la Candelaria. (See photograph on page 78.)

2 packages active dry yeast
1 cup warm water (about 110°)
    About 5¼ cups all-purpose flour, unsifted
¼ cup instant non-fat dry milk
1 cup (½ lb.) butter or margarine (at room temperature)
½ cup granulated sugar
1 teaspoon salt
3 eggs
½ cup *each* raisins and chopped walnuts
¼ cup chopped candied cherries
1 tablespoon *each* grated orange peel and lemon peel
3 tablespoons half-and-half (light cream) or whipping cream
2 cups sifted powdered sugar
½ teaspoon vanilla
    Candied fruits and nuts

In a large bowl, dissolve yeast in warm water. Add 1¼ cups of the flour and dry milk; beat well with a wooden spoon for 2 to 3 minutes. Cover and leave in a warm place about 30 minutes.

Meanwhile, in a separate bowl, cream butter with granulated sugar and salt. Beat in eggs, one at a time; add to yeast mixture; beat for about 3 minutes. Gradually stir in 3¾ cups of the flour.

Turn out dough on lightly floured board and knead until smooth and elastic (about 8 minutes); place in greased bowl. Turn over to grease top; cover and allow to rise in a warm place until nearly doubled in bulk (about 1½ hours).

Combine raisins, walnuts, cherries, orange and lemon peel. Pat dough out to about a 10-inch round on a floured board; top with fruit-nut mixture. Fold up edges of dough and knead in fruit and nuts until evenly distributed.

Divide dough in half; form each half into a long roll (about 20 inches); join ends of each roll to form rings and place each on greased baking sheet. Cover and allow to rise about 30 minutes. Bake in a 400° oven for 25 to 30 minutes or until bread sounds hollow when tapped. Cool baked loaves; cut out a small triangle from top of one and insert a tiny doll (see note following); replace wedge.

Stir together half-and-half, powdered sugar, and vanilla. Drizzle evenly over loaves. Decorate with "jewels" of candied fruits and nuts, left whole or sliced attractively. Makes 2 ring-shaped loaves.

Note. In Mexico a tiny china doll is usually baked right in the loaf. However, you may have trouble finding a china doll small enough and have to settle for a plastic one which would, of course, melt during the baking. Therefore the preceding method of inserting the doll is recommended. The sugar glaze will completely disguise where you have hidden it.

Desserts and Drinks

A showy olé

Luscious puddings and custards are the most characteristic desserts of Mexico. The flavoring may be cinnamon, almond, caramel, fruit, or cheese. Bread or even corn may be used for the most robust versions.

The variety of such sweets is attributed to the Spanish nuns, who vied among themselves to produce interesting new treats for special occasions and religious holidays, or to honor visiting dignitaries. Some of the classic dishes, sweet and otherwise, originated this way.

Other typical desserts are pastries, such as the deep-fried puffs or spirals—buñuelos or churros.

For any time of day you can find a special Mexican drink—breakfast chocolate, afternoon sangria cooler, before dinner cocktail, or a sipping dessert. Milk, wine, and fruit juices form the base for both hot and cold beverages. Most reflect the Mexican partiality for sugar and spice with an emphasis on cinnamon and chocolate.

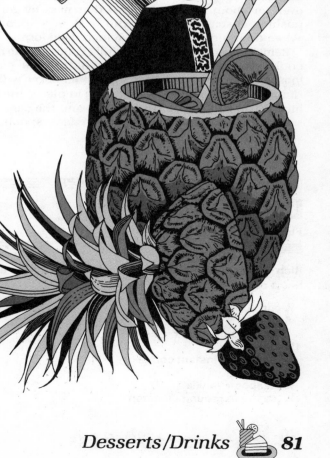

Caramel Custard

Flan (flahn)

Golden egg custard, baked in its own caramel sauce, is a classic sweet also served all over Europe and the Middle East. In Spain and Mexico it's called "flan."

- ⅓ **cup sugar**
- 6 **eggs**
- 6 **tablespoons sugar**
- 2 **cups milk**
- 1 **teaspoon vanilla**

Make a hot water bath for the flan by setting a 9 by 1¼-inch-deep pie pan in a slightly larger pan. While holding down metal pie pan so it won't float, fill outer pan with just enough hot water to come up around pie pan. Then remove pie pan and put only pan of water in a preheating 350° oven while you mix custard.

In a small frying pan over medium heat, melt the 1/3 cup sugar. To melt evenly, shake and tilt frying pan rather than stir sugar. Once melted, sugar will caramelize quickly; as soon as it does, pour immediately into the pie pan. Using hot pads to protect hands, tilt pie pan quickly to let syrup flow over bottom and slightly up sides. If syrup hardens before you finish, set pan on medium heat until syrup softens, then continue.

Beat together to blend eggs and the 6 tablespoons sugar; add milk and vanilla. Set caramel-lined pan in hot water in oven; pour in egg mixture. Bake in a 350° oven for about 25 minutes; test doneness by gently pushing custard in center with back of a spoon— when done a crevice about 3/8 inch deep forms.

Remove from hot water and chill at once. As the flan cools, caramel dissolves somewhat. When cold, loosen custard edge with a knife, then cover with a rimmed serving plate. Holding plate in place, quickly invert. The flan will slowly slip free and the caramel sauce flow out. To serve, cut in wedges, spoon on sauce. Makes 6 servings.

Coffee Flan

Flan de Cafe (flahn deh kah-*feh*)

Rich, coffee flavored custard, a variation of flan, also has a caramel topping.

- ⅓ **cup sugar**
- 6 **eggs**
- 7 **tablespoons sugar**
- 1½ **cups milk**
- 4 **teaspoons instant coffee**
- ½ **cup water**
- ½ **teaspoon vanilla**
- ¼ **teaspoon ground cinamon**

Make a hot water bath, melt the 1/3 cup sugar, and coat pie pan according to directions in preceding caramel custard recipe.

Beat together eggs and the 7 tablespoons sugar. Add milk, instant coffee dissolved in water, vanilla, and cinnamon. Set caramelized-sugar-lined pan in hot water bath in oven; pour in egg mixture. Bake in a 350° oven for 20 minutes or until a crevice about 3/8 inch deep forms when you gently push custard with back of a spoon at a point halfway between pan rim and center of pan. Remove pan from hot water bath; chill. When cold, loosen custard edge with a knife. Cover pan with a rimmed plate and hold together; invert flan onto plate. Makes 6 servings.

Almond Pudding

Almendrado (al-men-*drah*-thoh)

Mexicans love color, and this is evident even in their desserts. Pink, green, and white meringue puffs are served with a richly flavored almond sauce poured over all. (See photograph at right.)

- 1 **envelope unflavored gelatin**
- ¼ **cup cold water**
- 5 **eggs**
- ¾ **cup sugar**
- ½ **teaspoon almond extract**
- ¼ **teaspoon grated lemon peel**
  Red and green food coloring
  Almond custard sauce (recipe follows)

Sprinkle gelatin into cold water; let stand 5 minutes to soften, then place over hot water until dissolved. Separate eggs, placing whites in large bowl (reserve yolks for almond custard sauce; instructions follow). Add gelatin to egg whites.

Beat whites with electric mixer at highest speed until they form a thick, white foam. Continue beating and add sugar, no more than 1 tablespoon per minute, sprinkling it gradually over mixing whites. When whites form soft, curving peaks, add almond extract and lemon peel and beat in thoroughly.

Tint 1/3 of the meringue pale pink with a few drops of red food color, and tint another 1/3 of meringue pale green with a few drops of green food color. Pile pink, white, and green meringue mixtures side by side in a shallow bowl and chill, at least 2 hours or as long as 6 hours. With a cap of foil, cover meringue without touching it (it is easily marred).

(Continued on page 84)

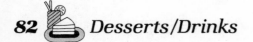

Spoon meringue into dessert bowls and pour almond custard sauce over each serving. Makes about 6 servings.

Almond custard sauce. In top of double boiler blend thoroughly 5 **egg yolks,** 1/4 cup **sugar,** 2 cups **milk,** and 1/4 teaspoon grated **lemon peel.** Cook, stirring constantly, over gently simmering water until mixture thickens enough to coat back of a metal spoon with a velvety layer. (If there is any sign of graininess at any time, remove custard from heat at once and set in cold water, stirring to cool quickly.)

Add 1/4 teaspoon **almond extract** and 3/4 cup toasted **slivered almonds** to custard, then set pan in cold water and stir to cool. Cover and chill (as long as overnight).

Mexican Meringue Cake with Strawberries

Torta de Merengue con Fresas
(*tor*-ta deh me-*ren*-geh kohn *freh*-sahs)

Three-inch-high wedges of billowy meringue cake, frosted with whipped cream, are served with strawberries. Since meringues require low oven temperature, it is wise to double-check your oven with a mercury oven thermometer.

- **5 egg whites**
- **½ teaspoon cream of tartar**
- **1 cup sugar**
- **1 teaspoon vanilla**
- **1½ cups whipping cream**
- **3 tablespoons Cointreau or other orange-flavored liqueur (or 1½ teaspoons vanilla)**
- **4 to 5 whole strawberries**
- **Sliced strawberries, sweetened to taste with sugar**

Use a clean, dry mixer bowl that holds at least 6 cups below top curve of beaters; in it, combine egg whites and cream of tartar. Beat whites at highest speed just until frothy (no bottom layer of free-flowing viscous white). Continue beating and add sugar, no more than 1 tablespoon per minute, sprinkling it gradually over mixing whites. When all sugar is incorporated, add vanilla and beat for 1 or 2 more minutes. Whites should hold very stiff, sharp, unbending peaks.

Evenly spread meringue in a greased and flour-dusted, deep, 8-inch cheesecake pan (one with removable bottom or spring released sides). Bake in a 275° oven for 1½ hours or until surface no longer feels sticky. Remove cake from oven and place on wire rack; immediately run knife blade around edge of pan to loosen cake. Let cake cool in pan 5 minutes; then remove pan sides. Cool 5 minutes longer; then invert onto a serving plate. Run a long metal spatula between pan base and cake and lift off base; let cake cool at room temperature (the shape is irregular).

Beat cream until stiff; stir in Cointreau. Spread whipped cream smoothly over top and sides of cake, correcting imperfections in symmetry of cake. Garnish with whole strawberries.

Serve at once or keep cold up to 1½ hours. Cut into wedges; pass a bowl of sliced, sugared strawberries to spoon over each serving. Makes 6 to 8 servings.

Mango Cream

Crema de Mango (*kreh*-mah deh *mahn*-goh)

Easily prepared but festive in appearance, this sweet fruit dessert offers interesting contrasts of texture.

Fresh mangoes are ripe when slightly soft (about the same "feel" as a ripe avocado or papaya).

- **5 large ripe mangoes, or 2 cans (14 oz. *each*) mangoes, drained**
- **Sugar**
- **2 oranges, peeled, seeded, and cut in small pieces**
- **1 tablespoon lemon juice**
- **2 cups (1 pt.) whipping cream**
- **1 cup pecan pieces**
- **12 green maraschino cherries**

Peel fresh mangoes; whirl mangoes in blender until smooth. Add sugar to taste (Mexicans like it sweet). Stir in oranges and lemon juice. Whip cream and fold into mango mixture. Add pecans. Serve in parfait glasses. Top each with a green cherry. Serves 12.

Baked Pineapple, Natillas

Piña al Horno con Natillas
(*pee*-nya *lor*-no kohn nah-*tee*-yas)

Hot baked pineapple, served from its leafy pineapple shell, is topped with a chilled custard sauce. (See photograph on page 38.)

- **1 large or 2 medium-size pineapples**
- **Sugar**
- **2 or 3 tablespoons rum or 1 teaspoon rum flavoring**
- **¼ cup butter or margarine**
- **Natillas sauce (recipe follows)**

Lay pineapple on its side and take off a thick slice (from one side) that does not include green top. Carefully scoop out fruit and cut into bite-size pieces. (Or, if you prefer, stand pineapple up, cut off its top, and remove the meat.)

Mix pineapple pieces with sugar to taste. Flavor with rum. Put pineapple pieces back into pineapple shell. Dot with butter, cover with foil (including

green leaves), and bake in a 350° oven for 20 minutes. Replace top and bring pineapple to the table on a plate to serve warm, topped with cold natillas sauce. Makes 8 to 12 servings.

Natillas sauce. Stir together 2 cups **half-and-half** (light cream), 1/4 teaspoon **salt**, 1/4 cup **sugar** beaten with 1 whole **egg** and 2 **egg yolks**, 2 teaspoons **cornstarch**, and 1 teaspoon **vanilla**. Cook over low heat, stirring constantly to avoid curdling, until smooth and slightly thickened (takes about 10 minutes). Chill.

Mexican Bread Pudding

Capirotada (kah-pee-roh-*tah*-tha)

Old-fashioned bread pudding, Mexican-style, is chock-full of cheese, apples, raisins, and nuts.

- 1 cup firmly packed brown sugar
- 1 cup water
- 1 cinnamon stick, 3 inches long
- ½ loaf (1-lb. size) French bread
- ½ cup *each* toasted pine nuts, toasted slivered almonds, and chopped walnuts
- 1 cup raisins
- ½ pound jack cheese, cut in ½-inch cubes
- 1 tart apple, thinly sliced
   Vanilla ice cream or whipped cream

Boil brown sugar, water, and cinnamon until slightly thickened (about 5 minutes). Discard cinnamon stick.

Cut bread into 1/2-inch-thick slices and toast; then break into large pieces. Place half the bread in a greased 9 by 13-inch baking dish. Add half the pine nuts in a layer, repeat with half the almonds, walnuts, raisins, and cheese in layers; top with all the sliced apple. Pour half the cinnamon syrup over all. Repeat layers and top with remaining syrup. Cover and bake in a 350° oven for about 15 minutes or until heated through (remove cover for last 5 minutes). Serve warm. To reheat, cover and bake in a 350° oven for about 15 minutes.

Spoon into individual dishes and top with vanilla ice cream or whipped cream. Makes 8 to 10 servings.

Flour Tortilla Torte

Torta de Tortillas de Harina
(*tor*-ta deh tor-*tee*-yahs deh ah-*ree*-nah)

This unorthodox dessert is remarkably easy to assemble. Its sour cream chocolate sauce is layered between flour tortillas. Plain sour cream frosts the surface, and chocolate curls add the final fillip. Cut into wedges to serve.

- 1 package (6 oz.) semisweet chocolate bits
- 2 cups (1 pt.) sour cream
- 3 tablespoons powdered sugar
- 4 flour tortillas (page 74 or purchased)
- 1 to 2 ounces milk chocolate

Pour semisweet chocolate bits into top of double boiler. Add 1 cup of sour cream and 1 tablespoon of the powdered sugar and heat over simmering water, stirring until chocolate is melted. Place pan of sauce in cold water to cool; stir occasionally.

Set one of the flour tortillas on a serving plate and spread evenly with a third of the chocolate mixture. Cover with another tortilla, another third of the sauce, then a third tortilla, the balance of the sauce, and the last tortilla. Make as level as possible.

Blend remaining sour cream with remaining 2 tablespoons powdered sugar and spread evenly over top and sides of the tortilla torte. Chill, covered with a large inverted bowl, at least 8 hours or as long as overnight.

Shave milk chocolate into curls using a vegetable peeler; pile chocolate curls onto top of tortilla torte. To serve, cut in slim wedges with a sharp knife. Makes 8 to 12 servings.

Milk Pudding

Leche Quemada (*leh*-cheh keh-*mah*-tha)

Dulce de leche, which means "sweet milk," and leche quemada, or "burnt milk," are both names for this dessert. The second name may refer to what can—but shouldn't—happen when dessert is being cooked for 5 or 6 hours to make it thick and caramel-colored. More likely, however, the word "burnt" may refer to the caramel quality, as caramel is sometimes called burnt sugar.

(Continued on page 87)

Cut pudding surface into even, 1 to 2-inch squares using a ruler as a guide and a sharp knife to cut straight down.

Pudding cooks slowly for 6 hours to form firm, white squares.

Serve tender cheese pudding squares with a thin cinnamon-flavored syrup (recipe at right).

The dessert is so rich that you should serve it in tiny containers, such as cordial glasses, nut cups, or small teacups.

- 1 quart milk
- 2 cups sugar
- 1 teaspoon vanilla or drop of almond extract (optional)
- Chopped nuts (optional)

In a 2-quart pan over high heat, bring milk and sugar to a full boil. (For darker, more caramel-like pudding, substitute 1/4 cup brown sugar for an equal amount of regular sugar.) Immediately reduce heat to low, and cook, uncovered; mixture should bubble gently; stir occasionally.

When it takes on a caramel color and thickens to consistency of a caramel topping or thin pudding (this will take 5 to 6 hours), remove from heat and cool. Flavor with vanilla or almond extract, if you wish.

Set in freezer or refrigerator to chill (in freezer it becomes a little firmer). It keeps a week in the refrigerator or freezer. If you like, top with chopped nuts. Makes 8 servings (3 tablespoons are sufficient for 1 serving).

Cheese Pudding in Syrup

Chongos Zamoranos (*chohn*-gos sah-*moh*-*rah*-nos)

Chongos, meaning "little knots," are tender, sweet pudding squares with a faint caramel flavor and cheeselike consistency. (In fact, the technique for preparing them resembles that for cottage cheese.)

The photographs on the opposite page show you how to cut the pudding into squares once it has set. A little care in cutting will produce attractive results.

Chongos cook for about 6 hours, but require little attention other than checking the rate of cooking. Then you transfer the chongos to a spicy syrup; this makes them firmer and adds flavor.

- 2 quarts milk
- 4 rennet tablets, finely crushed
- 4 tablespoons cold water
- ¾ cup sugar
- 3 teaspoons vanilla
- 2 cinnamon sticks, each 3 inches long, broken into smaller lengths
- 1 cup sugar
- 2 cups water or chongos liquid

In a 2½ to 3-quart pan, heat milk until lukewarm (110° on a deep-fat frying thermometer). Mix rennet with the 4 tablespoons water, the 3/4 cup sugar, and vanilla, and stir thoroughly into milk. Let stand, undisturbed, at room temperature for 1 hour or until set.

Note: If milk does not set, it has been heated to the wrong temperature, either too hot or not hot enough.

If setting does not occur the first time, reheat milk, adding 4 more rennet tablets, and repeat process.

Divide surface evenly into 1 to 2-inch squares, (smaller pieces make firmer chongos; larger pieces are softer in texture). Use a ruler and a thin, sharp knife; gently cut straight downward (be careful not to mar pan bottom) along edge of ruler.

Set pan on lowest heat and cook, uncovered, for 6 hours; mixture should never get hot enough to cause motion in pan as this will break up squares. *Do not stir*. After 6 hours, chongos should be white and as firm as warm cream cheese.

Combine cinnamon and the 1 cup sugar with the 2 cups water or chongos liquid (drain or siphon out the 2 cups with a bulb baster, disturbing the chongos as little as possible, then pour liquid through a cloth to remove scraps; add water if necessary to make 2 cups liquid). Bring to a boil in a deep pan; boil, uncovered, 5 minutes.

With a slotted spoon, gently transfer chongos to the hot syrup. Let stand in syrup until lukewarm before serving, or chill. (To store, cover and refrigerate up to 2 weeks.) To serve, spoon several chongos and some of the syrup into individual bowls. Makes 5 to 6 servings.

Coconut Candy

Dulces de Coco (*dool*-ses deh *koh*-koh)

This white fondant candy often is tinted bright green or a deep pink.

- 1 coconut or 2 cups shredded coconut and 2 cups canned or frozen coconut milk
- Water
- 4 cups sugar
- Food coloring (optional)

Make holes in the eyes of coconut; drain and reserve liquid. Crack coconut; remove brown husk and finely shred meat to make 2 cups. Set shredded coconut aside.

Add enough water to coconut liquid to make 2 cups (or use purchased coconut milk). Place coconut liquid mixture and sugar in a pan, and cook over high heat, stirring until mixture is clear. Wipe syrup spatter from pan sides with a brush dipped in water. Continue to cook, without stirring, on high heat until temperature is 240° on a deep-fat frying thermometer; wipe pan sides once or twice with wet brush.

Immediately remove pan from heat, wipe pan sides again, and quickly place the thermometer where syrup is to be poured. Pour syrup onto marble slap or into a ceramic tray or platter that is at least 10 by 12 inches, making sure to cover tip of thermometer; *do not scrape pan*.

Let stand undisturbed until cooled to at least 110° or

 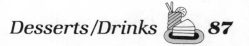

no colder than 90° (if thermometer is not in syrup, get an accurate reading by tipping it or turning it face down to immerse mercury bulb, then check). Avoid movement in syrup as much as possible, or it may become grainy.

Stir cooled syrup with a firm metal spatula or wooden paddle, agitating it quickly and continuously until it turns opaque and thickens to a firm, plastic mass that does not readily adhere to your fingers when lightly touched (about 10 to 15 minutes). Cover with waxed paper, invert a bowl over top and let stand until softened (about 15 minutes). Work mass with your hands in a kneading motion until it is glistening and smooth. (If you wish, kneaded candy can be made ahead, and at this point stored in airtight container in cool place as long as 1 week.)

Place kneaded candy in top of double boiler; melt over hot water, stirring occasionally, until the consistency of whipping cream. Stirring as little as possible, add reserved shredded coconut and enough food coloring to tint mixture to the desired color.

If more than one color is desired, divide melted candy into three parts and leave one part white; tint second part bright green and third part pink. Drop candy by teaspoonfuls onto wax paper; cool until hardened. Store airtight. Makes about 9 dozen candies.

Mexican Tea Cakes

Pasteles de Boda (pahs-*te*-lehs deh *bo*-tha)

Rich, buttery, Mexican tea (wedding) cakes are actually cookies. While still warm, they are thickly coated with powdered sugar. (See photograph on page 83.)

1½ cups butter or margarine, at room temperature
2 tablespoons powdered sugar
1 egg yolk
½ cup coarsely grated or finely chopped almonds
About 3½ cups all-purpose flour, unsifted
About 1 pound powdered sugar

Beat butter until light and fluffy; beat in the 2 tablespoons powdered sugar, egg yolk, and almonds. Gradually add flour to make a soft dough that you can shape with your hands. Pinch off pieces of dough the size of a large walnut and roll between your hands into round balls or form half moons. Place about 1½ inches apart on ungreased baking sheets and bake in a 275° oven 45 minutes or until very lightly browned. Remove from oven and let cool on baking sheets until lukewarm. Sift about ½ of the 1 pound powdered sugar over butcher paper, arranged in a shallow pan, and carefully transfer cookies from baking sheet to sugar. Sift more powdered sugar over tops and sides, completely coating cookies at least 1/8 inch thick with

sugar. Let stand until cool; store in an airtight container with waxed paper between layers of cookies. Makes about 2½ dozen.

Fluted Fritters

Churros
(*choo*-rrohs)

Street vendors in Mexico fry long fluted spirals of pastry called churros in great cauldrons of hot oil. When the airy-textured pastries are crisp and golden brown, the vendor sprinkles them with sugar and breaks them into short pieces to be sold. They're eaten still warm in nearby cafes for a light breakfast or after-supper snack with cups of hot chocolate or coffee.

Churros are easy to make at home. To give them the characteristic fluted appearance, you'll need a pastry bag or cooky press fitted with a star tip. The dough is similar to that of a cream puff. You squeeze it through the pastry tube directly into the hot oil, and as it fries, it swells to a crisp shell with a hollow interior. The warm churros are usually sprinkled with anise-flavored powdered sugar, but you can also sprinkle them with plain powdered or granulated sugar. (See photograph on page 94.)

2 teaspoons anise seed (optional)
½ cup powdered sugar, sifted
1 cup water
¼ teaspoon salt
1 teaspoon granulated sugar
½ cup (¼ lb.) butter or margarine
1 cup all-purpose flour, unsifted
4 eggs
¼ teaspoon lemon extract
Salad oil

If you use anise seed, slightly crush it and combine with powdered sugar at least 24 hours before you plan to make churros. Cover tightly and let stand; before using, sift sugar several times and discard seeds.

In a pan combine water, salt, granulated sugar, and butter; heat until butter melts. Bring to a full rolling boil over high heat, add flour all at once, remove pan from heat, and beat mixture with a spoon until it becomes a smooth, very thick paste that clings together and comes away from sides of pan. Add eggs, one at a time, beating well after each addition until paste is smooth and shiny.

Stir in lemon extract and let cool for 15 minutes. If you wish, paste can be covered and refrigerated at this point to fry later; let it warm to room temperature before using.

Fill a large pastry bag (fitted with a large star, or plain tip if you don't care about fluted look) with half the paste at a time; or fill a large cooky press with all of the paste. Heat 1 to 1½ inches salad oil in a wide frying pan to 400° on a deep-fat frying thermometer. Start squeez-

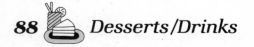

ing paste into oil until you have a ribbon of paste about 7 to 9 inches long; cut it off with a small knife. (You can fry 2 or 3 of these ribbons at a time.) Fry for 5 to 7 minutes, turning as needed, until well browned on all sides. With a slotted spoon, lift churros out of oil and drain on paper towels.

While churros are still warm, sprinkle with anise-flavored or plain sugar. Serve immediately. Makes about 1½ dozen churros.

"Pants" Biscuits

Calzones (kahl-*soh*-nehs)

This rolled dough makes a bland sweet biscuit, much like the popular American sugar cooky, which is cut into the shape of a pair of pants.

⅔ cup solid shortening, butter, or margarine
½ cup sugar
4 cups all-purpose flour, unsifted
5 teaspoons baking powder
1 teaspoon salt
1¼ cups milk
¼ cup sugar
¼ teaspoon ground cinnamon

Cream shortening and the 1/2 cup sugar until fluffy. Stir together flour, baking powder, and salt. Gradually add dry ingredients to creamed mixture alternately with milk, mixing until blended. Roll out dough on lightly floured board to 1/4-inch thickness.

With a sharp-pointed knife, cut out a piece of dough with a base 1¾ inches wide, sides 2¼ inches high, and top 1½ inches wide. Cut a small V-shaped wedge from middle of base. Repeat for each biscuit.

Place biscuits slightly apart on a greased baking sheet. Mix together the 1/4 cup sugar and cinnamon. Sprinkle over biscuits. Bake in a 350° oven for 15 to 20 minutes or until light brown. Makes about 5 dozen.

Fresh Prickly Pear Dessert

Postre de Tunas (*pos*-tre deh *too*-nas)

Prickly pear is the general term for the edible fruit of certain cactus. Beneath the treacherous, thorny skin of the prickly pear is sweet pulp which can make an intriguing dessert that is easy to prepare.

If you live in a warm, dry climate, you may have a prickly pear plant in your own yard. If not, look for the fruit in your produce market or a Mexican grocery in the fall.

The prickly pears you'll find in the market are usually pretty well denuded of their reddish brown, bristly spines. But to pick them from a cactus plant requires special care. Wear heavy leather gloves, or use several thicknesses of paper toweling or newspaper to grasp the fruit, then cut it off with a long knife.

To prepare the fruit in the kitchen, hold with tongs and rinse under cold running water. Lay on a plate or cutting board, still holding with tongs or a fork. Cut off both ends of the fruit, slit the skin remaining on fruit lengthwise, loosen and lay it back. Lift out the pulp.

Flavors of the various prickly pears differ somewhat, but all have a pleasing, fruity quality when ripe. They're delicious eaten as they are, as a fresh fruit.

For a simple dessert, slice large pieces of the fruit pulp into a sherbet glass, sweeten with sugar if desired, top with sweetened whipped cream, stick a lime wedge onto the glass rim, and squeeze the lime juice over as you eat.

Buñuelos

(boo-*nyue*-los)
Fried Sweet Puffs

Crisp, puffy rounds of sugar and cinnamon coated buñuelos make tasty accompaniments for sangria or coffee. (See photograph on page 91.)

4 eggs
¼ cup sugar
About 2 cups all-purpose flour, unsifted
1 teaspoon *each* baking powder and salt
Salad oil
1 cup sugar
1 teaspoon ground cinnamon

In bowl of an electric mixer, beat together eggs and the 1/4 cup sugar until thick and lemon colored. Stir together 1½ cups of the flour, baking powder, and salt; gradually add to egg mixture, beating until well blended; stir in an additional 1/4 cup flour. Turn soft dough out onto a board coated with about 1/4 cup flour; knead gently, working in as little flour as necessary, until dough is smooth and no longer sticky (about 5 minutes).

Divide dough into 16 equal pieces. With floured hands, shape each piece into a ball; cover balls with waxed paper as they are formed to prevent drying. When all balls are made and covered, allow to rest 20 to 25 minutes.

On a floured board, roll each ball out to make a 5-inch circle; stack circles, separating them with pieces of waxed paper as they're rolled.

Place 1½ inches of salad oil in a pan (at least 10-inch

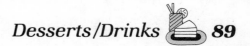

Desserts/Drinks **89**

diameter); heat oil to 350° on a deep-fat frying thermometer.

Meanwhile, mix together the 1 cup sugar and cinnamon. Sprinkle mixture into a 9-inch round cake pan. Using tongs, push circles of dough, one at a time, into hot oil and cook, turning once, until golden brown (about 1½ minutes). Remove from oil and drain briefly; place buñuelos in cinnamon-sugar mixture, turning to coat thoroughly.

Repeat until all buñuelos are cooked; reserve any leftover cinnamon-sugar mixture. Serve crisp pastries immediately; or cool completely and store in airtight containers at room temperature for as long as 3 days (freeze for longer storage).

To recrisp, arrange buñuelos in double layers on shallow, rimmed baking sheets. Bake, uncovered, in a 350° oven for 6 to 8 minutes or until hot; sprinkle with any leftover cinnamon-sugar mixture. Stack and serve warm or cooled on a large platter. Makes 16 pastries.

Coconut-Lime Drinks

Bebidas de Coco y Limon
(beh-*bee*-thas deh *koh*-koh ee lee-*mohn*)

Delicious coconut milk drinks with lime and tropical fruit juices are often served in Mexico. This surprises some tourists who think of such concoctions as Polynesian only.

    2 cups canned or frozen coconut milk, or
        home-prepared coconut milk (directions
        follow)
    ½ cup fresh lime juice
        Canned guava nectar, papaya juice, or
        passion fruit nectar
        Sugar
        Rum (optional)

If you use frozen coconut milk, thaw it and whirl in a blender before mixing drinks.

To make milk from packaged coconut, combine 2⅔ cups *each* flaked coconut and cold milk; refrigerate 1 hour. Whirl in a blender for about 40 seconds. Strain through a double thickness of cheesecloth squeezing out 2 cups of milk.

To make fresh coconut milk, make holes in the eyes of coconut; drain and reserve liquid. Crack coconut; remove brown husk and cut meat in 1/2-inch cubes (you should have about 2 cups). Place cubes in a blender and add 2⅔ cups hot liquid (obtained by adding enough hot water to coconut liquid to make necessary amount). Whirl coconut meat and hot liquid in blender for 20 to 30 seconds, then steep 30 minutes. Strain through a double thickness of cheesecloth, squeezing out about 2 cups milk.

Pour orange sangria (recipe below) over ice and garnish with fresh orange wedges. Crisp, cinnamon-sugar-sprinkled buñuelos (page 89) make perfect accompaniments.

With the 2 cups coconut milk and 1/2 cup fresh lime juice, you can make the following drinks by adding the specified amounts of juice, sugar, and rum. Serve each over ice immediately after mixing.

Coconut-guava. Combine the **coconut milk** and **lime juice** with 6 cups (four 12-oz. cans) **guava nectar**, 3/4 cup **sugar**, and 1 cup **rum**. Makes 8 servings.

Coconut-papaya. Combine **coconut milk** and **lime juice** with 2 cups (one 12-oz. can contains 1½ cups) **papaya juice**, 1/2 cup **sugar**, and 1/2 cup **rum**. Makes about 4 servings.

Coconut-passion fruit. Combine **coconut milk** and **lime juice** with 3 cups (two 12-oz. cans) **passion fruit nectar**, 1/2 cup **sugar**, and 1/2 cup **rum**. Makes about 5 servings.

Orange Sangria

Sangria de Naranja
(sahn-*gree*-ah deh nah-*ran*-hah)

Sangria, a red wine punch of Spanish origin, is served throughout Mexico, with or without food. Some versions contain lemon or lime juice, but this particular version—a very dark red punch made with orange juice—is one of the smoothest and most praiseworthy we've tasted. (See photograph on page 91.)

    1 medium-size orange
    ¼ cup sugar
    2 cups freshly squeezed or reconstituted frozen
        orange juice
    1 bottle (4/5 qt.) dry red wine
    ½ cup Cointreau (or other orange-flavored
        liqueur)
        Ice (optional)

Cut orange in half. Cut 4 thin slices from one half. Cut 2 slices into quarters; save for garnish. With a vegetable peeler, thinly cut off the thin outer peel of other half of orange. In a bowl, using a spoon, mash sugar into peel so sugar absorbs flavorful oils; then stir in orange juice, wine, and Cointreau. Cover and chill; after 15 minutes, remove orange peel.

Serve sangria in a bowl or from a pitcher, garnished with reserved orange slices. Add ice cubes to individual servings, if you like. Makes 6 cups, or 12 servings of 1/2 cup each.

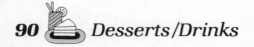

Lime Sangria Float

Sangria de Guadalajara
(sahn-*gree*-ah deh gooah-tha-la-*hah*-rah)

Guadalajarans make a beautiful sangria of red wine floating on a lime-flavored sparkling water base. Straws are inserted in the glass, and you may use them to sip from each layer or to swirl and blend.

      Sugar syrup (recipe follows)
1½ tablespoons lime juice
  ⅓ cup chilled sparkling water or club soda
      Ice cubes
  ½ cup chilled dry red wine

For each serving, use a glass that will hold at least 1½ cups. In glass, blend 2 tablespoons sugar syrup, lime juice, and chilled sparkling water. Drop in 4 or 5 ice cubes, then *carefully* pour chilled red wine onto ice; the wine will float in a distinct layer on the sparkling-water base.

Insert drinking straws and serve. Makes 1 serving.

Sugar syrup. Combine 1/2 cup *each* **sugar** and **water** in a pan and bring to a boil, stirring; cook until clear. Chill thoroughly. Makes about 2/3 cup, enough for 5 drinks.

Spicy Red Wine Punch

Ponche Rojo (*pon*-che *rro*-ho)

Serve hot punch in small mugs or cups. Spoon into each cup a few raisins, some apple slices, and a prune.

3½ quarts water
  3 cups sugar
  6 cinnamon sticks (*each* 3 inches long), broken
      in half
  3 medium-size Golden Delicious apples, peeled,
      cored, and cut into ¼-inch slices
  2 tablespoons lemon juice
  1 cup *each* raisins and whole pitted prunes
  2 quarts (64 oz.) dry red wine
  ¾ cup rum

In a 6-quart or larger pan, combine water, sugar, and cinnamon pieces. Bring to boiling over high heat; continue boiling rapidly until mixture is reduced to 3 quarts (about 15 minutes). Remove cinnamon pieces from syrup.

Meanwhile, mix apple slices with lemon juice to prevent browning. To syrup add apple-lemon juice mixture, raisins, prunes, and red wine; cover and chill if made ahead.

To serve, heat the wine mixture to steaming; remove from heat and stir in rum. Transfer to a heatproof serving bowl; ladle punch and several raisins, a prune, and a few apple slices into individual cups. Makes 12 to 16 servings.

Jamaica Punch

Ponche Jamaiquino (*pon*-che ha-mah-*kee*-noh)

The naturally bright-red color and sweet-tart flavor of Jamaica flower water make it similar to cranberry juice. Boil the dried Jamaica flowers or pods with water and sugar, let stand for a day, then strain and keep refrigerated in a pitcher for a tall, cool drink anytime; or use to make a sangria-style wine punch. You can find Jamaica flowers in Mexican grocery stores or large supermarkets carrying Mexican products.

  2 ounces (about 2 cups) dried Jamaica flowers
  6 cups water
1¼ cups sugar
      Ice
  1 bottle (4/5 qt.) well-chilled rosé
  1 bottle (16 oz.) well-chilled club soda
  1 orange, thinly sliced
  1 lemon, thinly sliced

In a 3-quart pan, combine Jamaica flowers, water, and sugar; bring to boil, reduce heat and simmer, uncovered, for 2 minutes. Transfer to a nonmetallic container; cover and chill at least 3 hours or until next day.

Pour Jamaica mixture through a wire strainer into a storage container; discard flowers. Cover and refrigerate up to 1 week.

For Jamaica flower drink, serve over ice. Makes about 1½ quarts.

For Jamaica flower punch, combine Jamaica flower drink with rosé and club soda in a 3 to 4-quart punch bowl, stirring to mix. Add chunk of ice; garnish with orange and lemon slices. Makes about 24 half-cup servings.

Tropical Fruit Punch

Ponche Tropical (*pon*-cheh troh-pee-*kal*)

A fragrant, soothing drink to accompany spicy dishes, this punch is made from four fruits—pineapple, orange, papaya, and guava—much enjoyed south of the border.

  4 to 8 slices fresh, peeled pineapple
  2 small oranges, peeled
  4 to 8 slices peeled and seeded papaya
1½ cups orange juice
  2 cans (12 oz. *each*) guava nectar
  4 mint sprigs

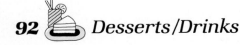

In each of 4 large glasses, arrange 1 or 2 slices pineapple, 1/2 orange (sliced), and 1 or 2 slices papaya.

Combine orange juice and guava nectar; pour evenly over fruit. Chill. Serve garnished with mint sprigs. Makes 4 servings.

Milk Punch

Ponche de Leche (*pon*-che deh *leh*-che)

The milk punch takes its inspiration from the Mexican milk-sugar sweet, cajeta. Start to make the punch ahead of time so it can chill, then serve with scoops of ice cream as a rich drink or dessert.

⅓ **cup sugar**
1 **quart milk**
1 **cinnamon stick (3 to 4 inches)**
Vanilla ice cream

In a 1½-quart pan, melt sugar over medium heat, tilting pan (rather than stirring to melt sugar evenly). When sugar is a rich amber color, pour milk into pan all at once (mixture foams vigorously). Add cinnamon stick and heat milk to scalding, stirring frequently. Cover and chill as long as 24 hours. Discard cinnamon stick.

To serve, spoon a scoop or two of vanilla ice cream into each serving glass and fill with milk mixture. Makes 4 to 6 servings.

Hot Chocolate

Chocolate Caliente (choh-koh-*lah*-teh kah-lee-*en*-teh)

Mexican hot chocolate is best made with rich milk, flavored with cinnamon and beaten until frothy. You can make it easily with squares of unsweetened chocolate, ground spice, and an electric or hand beater. But for authenticity and the sheer fun of it, buy Mexican chocolate and a typical wooden chocolate beater. (See photographs on pages 46 and 94.)

The chocolate is sold in cakes or pellets already containing the necessary sugar and cinnamon, and usually almonds and egg. The almonds provide flavor, and the egg produces more froth. These cakes are sold in bulk, or in packages labelled "Mexican confection." Since the labels make no mention of purpose or use for this chocolate, it is often placed mistakenly on grocery shelves along with candy.

The primitive chocolate beater (called a "molinillo") is a decoratively carved instrument which resembles a bass drum stick with grooves and loose wooden rings just above the knobby end to produce the froth. You put the end with knob and rings in the hot chocolate and hold the other slender end between your palms. Rub your palms together to twirl the beater—the way Indians once twirled a stick in a stone to strike sparks for starting a fire.

You may find molinillos in some import shops, as well as Mexican stores. Because they look so much like a toy, they too may be displayed in an unlikely section of the store.

For each 2 servings, use half of a 2-ounce cake of prepared **Mexican chocolate**, shaved (or a 1-oz. square of unsweetened chocolate, shaved; 1 tablespoon sugar; a pinch of salt; and 1/2 teaspoon ground cinnamon). Combine with 2 cups of **milk** and cook over hot water until chocolate melts. Beat until foamy and pour into cups; or pour into a pitcher and beat with the molinillo where your guests can watch.

Margaritas

(mar-ga-*ree*-tas)

Served in chilled, salt-rimmed stemware, margaritas are a popular, lime green, before-dinner drink made from the potent Mexican liquor, tequila (teh-*kee*-la).

Coarse salt
¾ **cup (6 oz.) tequila**
¾ **cup (6 oz.) triple sec**
¾ **cup (6 oz.) fresh lime juice**
About ¾ cup coarsely crushed ice

Thoroughly chill 4 stemmed glasses (about 1/2-cup size). Invert glass rims in coarse salt to coat evenly; set aside.

In a blender, combine tequila, triple sec, lime juice, and crushed ice. Whirl until frothy and well blended. Serve in salt-rimmed glasses. Makes 4 servings.

Churros—long, fluted, fritterlike pastry spirals (page 88)—go well with cinnamon-flavored hot chocolate (page 93). Traditional wooden chocolate beater is called a "molinillo."

Index

A Handy Metric Conversion Table

To change	To	Multiply By
ounces (oz.)	grams (g)	28
pounds (lb.)	kilograms (kg)	0.45
teaspoons	milliliters (ml)	5
tablespoons	milliliters (ml)	15
fluid ounces (oz.)	milliliters (ml)	30
cups	liters (l)	0.24
pints (pt.)	liters (l)	0.47
quarts (qt.)	liters (l)	0.95
gallons (gal.)	liters (l)	3.8
Fahrenheit temperature (°F)	Celsius temperature (°C)	5/9 after subtracting 32